At War with Waugh

by the same author

Dear Bill

At War with Waugh

The Real Story of *Scoop*

W. F. DEEDES

MACMILLAN

First published 2003 by Macmillan
an imprint of Pan Macmillan Ltd
Pan Macmillan, 20 New Wharf Road, London N1 9RR
Basingstoke and Oxford
Associated companies throughout the world
www.panmacmillan.com

ISBN 1 405 00573 4

5 7 9 8 6

A CIP catalogue record for this book is available from
the British Library.

Typeset by SX Composing DTP, Rayleigh, Essex
Printed and bound in Great Britain by
Mackays of Chatham plc, Chatham, Kent

At War with Waugh

One

One sunny morning early in August 1935, I was summoned from the *Morning Post*'s reporters' room by H. A. Gwynne, editor since 1911, and asked if I was willing to go as the newspaper's correspondent to Abyssinia, where war with Italy seemed inevitable. Gwynne had been a Reuters war correspondent in the South African war along with Winston Churchill, Edgar Wallace and others, and so had plenty of avuncular advice to offer. A dead correspondent, he reminded me cheerfully, was useless to his newspaper. A finger of whisky in the water bottle killed bugs in doubtful water. Above all, as a representative of the *Morning Post*, I must look the part, acquire the proper kit, and so on. Anxious to seem equal to the occasion, I nodded eagerly, but felt unable to contribute much to the conversation because at the age of twenty-two I had never travelled beyond Switzerland, had never been a war correspondent and knew nothing about Abyssinia.

Gwynne, observing my silence, thought I might wish to think over the offer. I promised to do so and put in a telephone call to my distinguished uncle, Sir Wyndham Deedes, whose residence in Bethnal Green's Victoria Park Square I shared.

After soldiering in the Boer War with the 60th Rifles, he had become an army interpreter in Turkish and Arabic, was appointed an intelligence officer at the Dardanelles and ended the 1914–18 war with Allenby and Lawrence of Arabia at Government House in Jerusalem. He received my news calmly, thought it was up to me to decide but saw no reason to refuse.

The *Morning Post* news editor, Mervyn Ellis, was manifestly relieved by my acceptance. He had, I surmised, recommended my name to Gwynne. In some respects I was a good candidate for such a venture, being young, unmarried, without dependants and easily insurable. After I had agreed to go, Ellis told me that the newspaper thought it likely that those reporting the war from the Abyssinian side would be cut off by the Italian advance, so I must be equipped to withstand a long siege. That line of thought led to a lively shopping spree.

At Austin Reed in Regent Street, where Ellis and I made most of our purchases, the notion of preparing me for an extended siege was greeted with enthusiasm. We were persuaded to buy, among other things: three tropical suits, riding breeches for winter and summer, bush shirts, a sola topi, a double-brimmed sun hat, a camp bed and sleeping bag, and long boots to deter mosquitoes at sundown. To contain some of these purchases we bought two large metal uniform cases and a heavy trunk made of cedar wood and lined with zinc to keep ants at bay.

Nobody seemed to know much about the climate except that it was highly variable. In the Somaliland and Danakil lowlands, one would encounter semi-tropical conditions. Addis

Ababa, where I was to go, was 8,000 feet above sea level with temperatures during most of the year no higher than an early English summer.

At the Army and Navy Stores in Victoria Street, we found a department that specialized in kitting out those bound for the tropics. They knew where Abyssinia was and could suggest the right medicines for the region. These included bottles of quinine pills which were then reckoned to be the best protection against malaria. The Army and Navy also produced slabs of highly nutritious black chocolate – an iron ration for emergencies to go inside the zinc-lined trunk. Our purchases in all weighed just short of 600 pounds – a quarter of a ton. I was not to know that such extravagance would contribute to Evelyn Waugh's portrait of William Boot in *Scoop*, the novel he later wrote about journalists covering the war.

There were other preparations to be made: a visa to be obtained from the Abyssinian embassy in London, a large sum of money to be drawn from the newspaper's bank and bookings to be made for the complicated journey to Addis Ababa which in those days occupied the best part of a fortnight. True to his word about travelling in style, Gwynne equipped me with an open letter, with a huge blue seal, informing all whom it may concern that Mr William Francis Deedes had been appointed special correspondent in Abyssinia, The Sudan, Somaliland and British East Africa, and requesting on his behalf all permissible facilities.

He also sent me a longer, personal letter which I treasure, for it carries the flavour of those less hurried days and reminds me what a kindly place the *Morning Post* was. After expressing touching confidence in my abilities, it continues dauntingly: 'As an old war correspondent myself, I realise that the difficulties that await a correspondent in Abyssinia are enormous. In the first place, there are two fronts – in the North, Eritrea, and, in the South, Italian Somaliland. Presumably, so far as one can make out, the attack in force will come from the North, but I have no doubt that the Italians will try to make a diversion from the South.' Gwynne was right on that count.

'One man,' he went on reasonably, 'can only be in one place at a time, and therefore it would be ridiculous to expect you to cover all the fighting – if fighting takes place – in Abyssinia. All I can suggest to you is that you should keep as near headquarters as you can, for there news of every engagement will ultimately arrive. By keeping in touch with general headquarters you will be sure to get all the big news as soon as anybody else.' Here he was wrong, for experience in the Boer War and the Great War offered no guidance at all for extracting news from the secretive and sometimes devious Abyssinian officials in Addis Ababa.

> '*I am not laying this down as a positive instruction,*' this letter on azure-blue writing paper continued, '*for obviously, you must be allowed a large amount of discretion, but from my own experience in this kind of open warfare, I have found it myself of great advantage to keep in general touch with GHQ. This does not*

preclude you from going wherever you think you can get the best copy.

'I do not know Abyssinia, though I have been very close to the borders, but I do know something about its climate. It is very hot in the plains and at Djibouti and you will, therefore, have to provide yourself with clothing for a tropical climate. At the same time, on the heights, the weather is cold and the wind keen and, therefore, you will have to make provision for those tremendous drops of temperature which occur in the Abyssinian highlands.' That was not so far off the mark.

'As regards financial arrangements, of course all your expenses will be charges on the office. In addition to that, I propose that, while you are acting as a Special Correspondent, you will have allocated to you, in addition to your present salary, a sum of £20 a month [about £800 in today's money], *and this additional remuneration can either accumulate here for you, or be sent to you, whichever you desire.*

'You will have to outfit yourself for the climate, with the knowledge that we have of it, and I hope you will observe due economy in getting an outfit.

'It will be necessary for you to get a visa from the Abyssinian Legation and, in order to do this, we shall have to deposit with the London office

of the Bank of Egypt the sum of £40, which will be refunded to you when you return. This part we can arrange, but you had better get in touch with the Legation, and let us know exactly the procedure we have to follow.

'In addition to other financial arrangements we are making, we are going to insure your life. Details of this will be given you before you leave.

'As regards telegraphing, here again we must leave it almost entirely to your discretion. We shall be glad to have anything you can send by mail, but we want to be on a level with our competitors in regard to telegrams. The length also, of such cables as you may send must be left to your discretion. While we do not want to be extravagant, yet we want to be in a position to give as good a picture as any other paper with one correspondent can give.

'I imagine there will be great difficulties in getting messages off. With the large number of correspondents, it should not be difficult to arrange a system of runners who could work for the whole corps of correspondents and thus save money and time.'

That final sentence, relating no doubt to Gwynne's recollection of the South African war, suggests that the cleft sticks which Waugh mentions in *Scoop* were not altogether fanciful.

'I need not assure you,' Gwynne's letter concluded, 'that I wish you every success, and I am quite sure that the experience you will gain as a Special Correspondent in Abyssinia will be of great value to yourself and to the paper hereafter.'

All things considered, it was a generous letter. The *Morning Post*'s grand days were behind it. It had left a fine office in Aldwych overlooking Waterloo Bridge, and was tenant of a property in Tudor Street (which runs parallel with Fleet Street) owned by its printers, the Argus Press. If I had received such a letter from my editor today, it might have given me a sleepless night. What troubled my mind then, to the exclusion of almost everything else, was how I might contrive to convey a quarter of a ton of luggage in six separate pieces from London to Addis Ababa.

While newspapers like the *Morning Post* made their preparations to cover the forthcoming war, ministers in London were wrestling with the infinitely harder task of averting it. Though seen against the huge tapestry of the Second World War as a relatively minor event, rendered faintly ridiculous by *Scoop*, Mussolini's attack on Abyssinia can now clearly be seen as a prelude to 1939–45. The British government's sincere but ill-starred efforts to stop Italian aggression failed, and that failure sent out all the wrong signals, particularly to Hitler. We pursued too many worthy but conflicting aims. Anxious to keep Mussolini on our side, we prevaricated, turning him into a deadly enemy. Desirous of upholding the authority of the fragile League of Nations, we made undertakings that we lacked the military strength to fulfil.

W. F. DEEDES

Mussolini's determination to establish military dominion over Abyssinia had been apparent from the start of 1935. At home, he was sorely in need of a triumph, and he had long been aggrieved by Italy's small share of the African spoils at the end of the First World War. Moreover, Italy's defeat by Abyssinia near Adowa in 1896, an encounter in which the Italians lost 4,500 white and 2,000 native troops killed and wounded, continued to rankle. As he had made abundantly clear at the Stresa conference in April 1935, Mussolini saw the peace of Europe as desirable, but peace in Africa a different matter altogether. Britain had noted this, but hesitated to pursue the question of Abyssinia with Mussolini at the time because we wanted his support for the Stresa agreement. This was signed by Britain, France and Italy in response to German rearmament, which Hitler had declared a month earlier. In theory the signatories undertook to defend Austria's independence from the threat of a forced *Anschluss* with Germany. In reality the agreement posed no serious threat to Germany's ambitions in Europe and collapsed six months later after Mussolini invaded Abyssinia.

The British government also set store by another agreement, contrived by the Admiralty, the Anglo-German naval treaty, which sought to limit the German fleet to a third of the British in return for which Germany was conceded the right to build U-boats – something explicitly denied her at the Treaty of Versailles. All this was arranged without consulting France, who felt that her vital interests had been ignored in granting Germany this concession.

The announcement of this ill-considered treaty had several

consequences, none of them favourable. It was seen as another, if indirect, setback to the League of Nations. Hitler had the satisfaction of seeing France and Britain divided on the question. Mussolini read it as a sign that by putting what she saw as her own naval interests first, Britain was not acting in good faith with her allies. 'He was,' Churchill observed in his history of the Second World War, 'encouraged by what seemed the cynical and selfish attitude of Great Britain to press on with his plans against Abyssinia.' The Scandinavian countries perceived that Britain had agreed to a German navy that would give Hitler mastery of the Baltic.

As if the stars were not already set in their course against British interests, we then had the result of the Peace Ballot. This had been sponsored and organized in the early months of 1935 by the League of Nations Union. In June 1935, Lord Cecil, who had been the moving spirit of the enterprise, announced the result to a meeting in the Albert Hall. Since most people have long since forgotten what the Peace Ballot was about, and because it had an impact on the thinking of ministers, it is well to set down the questions asked in full.

1. Should Britain remain a member of the League of Nations?
2. Are you in favour of an all-round reduction of armaments by international agreement?
3. Are you in favour of the all-round abolition of national military and naval aircraft by international agreement?

4. Should the manufacture and sale of armaments for private profit be prohibited by international agreement?
5. Do you consider that if a nation insists on attacking another, the other nations should combine to compel it to stop by:
   a. economic and non-military measures
   b. if necessary, military measures?

Over eleven million people responded to the ballot. Lord Cecil pointed out with great satisfaction that the affirmative answers to most of the questions outnumbered the votes ever given to any single party in any general election, save those given to the Conservative party in 1931, which had been an exceptional result.

Some charitably saw the Peace Ballot figures as underlining Great Britain's attachment to the League of Nations; others regarded it as part of a pacifist campaign. As a reporter at the time, I can affirm that in 1935 the desire for peace had a most powerful hold on the country. We had seen that at the East Fulham by-election in 1933, which had profoundly affected the pace at which Baldwin deemed it feasible to go about rearmament when it came to the General Election of 1935. A swing against the government of 26.5 per cent had been widely interpreted as a triumph for peace and disarmament.

Seen in the context of those times, this yearning for peace at almost any price was not in the least surprising. We were barely fifteen years away from the carnage of the First World War. Countless families had lost their menfolk; a lot of my mother's friends were war widows. As Hitler progressively flouted the terms of international undertakings and rearmed that mood began to change, but in the summer of 1935 we were dealing with the 'years that the locusts had eaten', in Baldwin's phrase to the House of Commons in November 1936; we were dealing with neglected defences.

Hopes of peace received their final blow, after Mussolini had invaded Abyssinia in October 1935, with the sudden awareness that Britain was poorly placed to take him on in the Mediterranean, if Italy decided to strike back against sanctions. Baldwin was at least realistic about sanctions. They meant war, he said. If you imposed them effectively, you had to be prepared to go to war. So sanctions against Italy had to stay short of anything that might provoke outright hostilities. A large number of commodities, some of which were war materials, were prohibited from entering Italy but, as I saw clearly enough as I passed through the Suez Canal on my way to Abyssinia, the oil continued to flow freely. To stop the oil would have brought Italy's campaign against Abyssinia to a halt. But that could have led to war. So it was not halted.

It resembled a game of poker, Mussolini's bluff against our bluff, but ultimately he faced us down – with grievous consequences. As Churchill put it in his history of the Second World War:

> Mussolini would never have dared to come to grips with a resolute British Government. Nearly the whole world was against him, and he would have had to risk his regime upon a single-handed

war with Britain . . . How could Italy have fought this war? Apart from a limited advantage in modern light cruisers, her navy was but a fourth the size of the British. Her numerous conscript Army . . . would not come into action. Her air power was in quantity and quality far below even our modest establishment. She would have been instantly blockaded. The Italian armies in Abyssinia would have been famished for supplies and ammunition . . . If ever there was an opportunity of striking a decisive blow in a generous cause with a minimum of risk, it was here and now. The fact that the nerve of the British Government was not equal to the occasion can be excused only by their sincere love of peace. Actually it played a part in leading to an infinitely more terrible war. Mussolini's bluff succeeded, and an important spectator drew far-reaching conclusions from the fact.

There is truth in that judgement, delivered more than a decade later, but it omits one important consideration. The British government in 1931-5 was still a coalition, which had been brought together at the behest of King George V to deal with the economic crisis that had befallen the country in 1931. With former members of the Liberal and Labour parties on board, it was frequently divided on the correct course to follow with Mussolini. The Labour party was also sharply divided. At its Brighton conference in October 1935, Ernest

Bevin, general secretary of the Transport and General Workers' Union, felt moved to exclaim harshly to George Lansbury, the party leader, '[You are] placing the Movement in an absolutely wrong position to be hawking your conscience round from body to body asking to be told what you ought to do with it.'

Mussolini caused feelings to run high in Britain – but in different directions. Neither Ramsey MacDonald nor Stanley Baldwin, who succeeded him as prime minister in June 1935, found it easy to keep faith with our allies, uphold the League of Nations, deter Mussolini, and avoid a war for which we were unready and which the public had made clear it did not want.

Abyssinia, moreover, was a member of the League of Nations; Italy had pressed for her inclusion in 1923. Britain, who felt that a country in which tribal war and slavery prevailed was an unsuitable candidate, had opposed it. Italy prevailed. Evelyn Waugh, who had attended the coronation of the Emperor Haile Selassie in 1930, made no secret of his views: he saw Abyssinia as a savage place which Mussolini was doing well to tame. But, as Churchill put it convincingly, Mussolini's designs upon Abyssinia were unsuited to the ethics of the twentieth century. 'They belonged to those dark ages when white men felt themselves entitled to conquer yellow, brown, black or red men, and subjugate them by their superior strength and weapons.' That indeed is what made the Abyssinian adventure so extraordinary. Mussolini was the last European leader to set about empire-building by the sword.

Two

None of these considerations weighed heavily on my mind as I left Victoria Station one hot August day on the first leg of my journey to Addis Ababa. There had been touching farewells at the *Morning Post* office, where several colleagues made it disturbingly clear that they did not expect to see me again. The chief reporter, S. R. Pawley, gave me his battered compass – property of the Territorial Army. A godmother invited me to spend a fiver on an expensive briefcase at the Army and Navy Stores, which brought the pieces of baggage I had to guard up to seven. It had taken two taxis to convey me and my gear from my uncle's house in Bethnal Green to the station.

Waugh's William Boot, occasional contributor of nature notes to Lord Copper's *Beast*, flew to Paris at the newspaper's expense and then caught the Blue Train to Marseilles. After they had weighed his luggage at Croydon he was called on to pay a supplement of £103 – about £4,000 in today's money – then they produced an additional aeroplane. The *Morning Post* couldn't quite run to that, but I was booked through on the Blue Train, which at that time conveniently ran direct from Calais to Marseilles. Those were the days when well-to-do people travelled with mountains of luggage, including unwieldy cabin trunks, so there were abundant porters at Marseilles to deal with my collection which with the help of a courier was stacked away in no time at all on the Messageries Maritimes steamship *General Metzinger* for the long sea voyage. Today's foreign room would have procured a visa for me, booked a seat on the next plane and had me filing copy from Addis Ababa within hours.

The *General Metzinger* being a French boat, the cuisine was a strength. A weakness was its second- and third-class cabins, in which the temperatures soared long before we reached the Red Sea. I shared a second-class cabin with a Turkish merchant named Alfred Roche who was travelling as far as Jaffa. I found the food exciting but strenuous. We were served in bed with a light meal at 7.30 and had a proper breakfast at 9 a.m., which left an interval of only three hours before a lunch of six courses. Nobody except the handful of English people on board took any exercise. Tea was served at 4.00 and a long dinner at 7 p.m.

I fell in with a Mexican of about thirty who belonged to a wealthy family, had found life too tame in America and was travelling around the world looking for trouble. He claimed to have been with the revolutionary forces in Cuba, to have joined Bolivia against Paraguay, and declared he had fought in four civil wars. As a qualified pilot whose recreation was also flying he had not found it difficult to persuade the Abyssinian legation in London to send him to Addis Ababa as an officer in the almost non-existent Abyssinian Air Force. It sounded an unlikely tale but, as I discovered later, some very strange people were making their way to the area with an eye to adventure and opportunity. The Spanish Civil War, which was to start a year later, drew people who wanted to fight fascism; Abyssinia's war attracted more mercenary characters. With the Mexican was an equally improbable character, a young Nazi who declared he had deserted his regiment in Berlin to fly for Abyssinia. He claimed to have flown 600 hours solo but, as the Mexican told me confidentially, this was unlikely because he suffered acutely from airsickness.

One of my saner companions was a man named Hunter, who had served in the Sudan government service. He kept his plans well concealed and I put him down as a minor dealer in armaments. The most congenial figure I encountered, a Mr Glass, was employed by Cable & Wireless and was travelling with his wife and young son to Mauritius. Various religious denominations were represented on board, and needed to be, for there was a tremendous mix of nationalities; services for one faith or another took place at all hours and interrupted deck sports.

At Port Said I had a stroke of luck. The port commandant had been a wartime friend of my Uncle Wyndham, who had cabled asking him to assist me. As we docked, a police launch came alongside, an English officer in a gorgeous fez saluted and then whisked me off the ship before anybody else had disembarked. He was, he explained, the second in command and responsible for Italian traffic through the Suez Canal. In return for my undertaking to file nothing that he told me from Port Said, he opened his records and gave me every encouragement to report what he said. In common with many British officials who knew what was going on, he seemed to think, rightly, that the Italians were getting away with murder.

The signs of war were unmistakable. I learned that six Italian ships carrying 15,000 men were at that point – the first week in September – in transit through the canal. All were bound for the east coast of Africa. My informant reckoned that 200,000 Italians had gone through, as well as thousands of tons of war material. An aircraft carrier, two submarines, two sloops and one light cruiser had passed through in the last few days. There were Italian ships moving west as well as east and they included three hospital ships returning with invalids. The number of sick was closely guarded, but the deputy commandant thought it already amounted to between ten and twelve thousand men. Among other blunders, Italian labourers had been put to work on building roads wearing sun hats without spinal pads and had been laid low by the tropical sun. A large hospital had been opened on the island of Rhodes – at that time controlled by Italy – which treated the afflicted and sent them back to Eritrea. There were Italian deserters too, and the Port Said authorities were nervous of trouble because there were already 70,000 Italians in Egypt to whom the local population was inclined to be hostile.

We discussed the cost of all this. The Italians were using passenger liners, and only three of the twelve Italian liners which plied this route now regularly carried civilians. Oiling alone was costing Italian ships passing through Suez £10,000 a month – about £500,000 in today's money. The Suez Canal Company tolls paid by the Italians were £100,000 up on the previous year.

All this made good copy. My difficulty was getting it back

to London without breaking my undertaking to wire nothing from Port Said. We were not stopping again before disembarking at Djibouti in French Somaliland. My resourceful friend, Mr Glass of Cable & Wireless, lent a hand. We stopped but did not land at Suez, where a Messageries Maritimes agent came on board to inspect the ship. He was persuaded to take my telegram to the manager of Eastern Telegraphs in Suez. Glass addressed a duplicate to a friend in Suez with instructions to take it at once to Eastern Telegraphs and transmit it if the first copy had not gone off. I am sometimes asked how we filed our copy in the days before international telephones and e-mail. It was often a nightmare, particularly as any feedback from the office was slow to arrive and one would spend a couple of nights or more wondering whether the copy had reached London.

By now it was fiercely hot and work of any kind unwelcome. The Glass boy, aged six and suffering from prickly heat, quarrelled with a French child and socked him on the jaw, which caused a minor uproar. It was that sort of ship and that sort of weather. I observed that at Port Said we had picked up fresh passengers. They included a man from the *Daily Mail*, four photographers and a bevy of American journalists among whom was Randolph Hearst's international correspondent, H. R. Knickerbocker, whom I knew by repute. His appearance cheered me up considerably; if he is on board, I thought, there is bound to be a war. Our ship's company now included five English journalists, six from France and one each from Belgium, Japan and Spain, all bound for Djibouti and thence Addis Ababa.

Familiar with the tropics, Glass counselled us all to drink iced lemon juice until sundown, when he treated himself to one large whisky and soda and later a second before going to bed. He was a creature of habit. Seeing a journalist drink a whisky and soda at teatime nearly broke his heart. He was not much over forty, but having lived for twenty years east of Suez he had white hair and looked about sixty. When we parted from him at Djibouti, he looked disconsolate, as well he might, for he faced another three weeks on board before reaching Mauritius.

Trains from Djibouti to Addis Ababa were infrequent. We were lucky in that we landed at the French port late on a Sunday evening and were able to catch a train early on Tuesday morning. Djibouti in those days was a hellhole, with its stupendous heat and shoddy hotels. It struck me as the sort of place where men who disgraced themselves in Somerset Maugham tales might wish to come and drink themselves to death. Drinking even lemon squash in Djibouti was hazardous because flies were everywhere and crowded greedily around every glass. I spent some of Monday visiting French and Abyssinian officials in the port. Even the prospect of war had not stirred their lethargy. The story I filed from there began: 'In the total absence of any reliable news whatever by newspapers, radio or other means of communication, the population of this town awaits developments in astonishing tranquillity . . .' It was not altogether surprising. We were in French Somaliland whereas most of the Italian ships were arriving higher up the coast at Massawa. Very little news filtered through from there.

The Abyssinian consul thought that about 180,000 Italian troops had landed on the coast and assured me that 5,000 of them had already deserted to Abyssinia. Scenting a spin doctor at work, I filed this intelligence cautiously. Of greater interest was the likely fate of the railway. There was virtually no other means of transport in or out of the capital except pack animal. If the railway were cut, one would be well and truly stuck in Addis Ababa. The governor of Djibouti was not altogether reassuring. The line, he explained, was well guarded in French Somaliland, but that was the limit of his responsibility. The Abyssinian consul was confident it would be cut but assured me that men were on hand to repair it. If the line was interrupted in more than one place a shuttle service would be run between the gaps, for which ample rolling stock was available. I did not find this cheering.

Very early on Tuesday morning I thankfully took the train out of Djibouti, where the midday temperature had risen to 110°F. The two representatives of Hearst Newspapers, Carl von Weigand and H. R. Knickerbocker, had secured the train's wagon-lit and invited me to join them. It was the first and last occasion I have travelled in a coach from which all but white people were excluded. With possession of the sleeping car and twelve bottles of iced Vichy water in two huge Thermos flasks, we were comfortably placed. Outside our car, conditions were primitive. The seats were hard, the loos elementary; food and drink were available only from vendors at station stops. Being the only means of reaching the capital on wheels, the railway could afford to be pretty offhand with its customers. Towards noon, Knickerbocker produced his whisky flask and poured some into his Vichy water. Von Weigand, a much older man, looked shocked and muttered, 'You'll kill yourself with that stuff.' Shades of Mr Glass of Cable & Wireless, I thought. Knickerbocker was in fact a moderate drinker, and anyway it was growing milder. We stopped on the line for lunch and slept the night at Dire Dawa, about halfway to Addis Ababa. At 2,000 feet it was markedly cooler. Told we were entering a malarial mosquito zone, I took a couple of my quinine tablets, which made my ears sing alarmingly.

Next morning the train left at 5.30 and we lunched at Awash. As the train climbed towards the highlands and the plateau on which Addis Ababa stands, I marvelled at the skill with which engineers had carved a route for this railway through such rugged territory. The great Emperor Menelik II had granted the first concession to a French company in 1894. The company encountered such difficulties and financial problems that the French government had come to the rescue and provided the necessary funds. That got the railway from the coast to Dire Dawa by 1902 and a good carriage road took the traveller on to Harar. Extending the line from Dire Dawa to Addis Ababa proved even more daunting; it was not until 1906 that an Anglo-French-Italian agreement was signed in London, and a French company contracted to do the work. I have travelled along it several times since, sometimes thinking to myself that it was the nineteenth rather than the twentieth century that produced the engineering wonders of the world.

We made one final stop forty miles outside Addis Ababa for refuelling. The Hearst correspondent in Addis Ababa had taken the train from Addis to greet his distinguished colleagues and had ordered a large cooked tea in the local hotel for them. We had just enough time to make a hole in the meal before the train started up again. Suddenly it began to rain torrentially and became rather cold. I thought wistfully of my tropical suits in the luggage van and wondered if Austin Reed had got it right. We were glad of the high tea, for the train did not reach Addis Ababa until nine o'clock that night. Stuart Emeny, a senior reporter on the *News Chronicle* I had come to know well from stories we had covered together in England, met the train with Evelyn Waugh and our own local man, Salmon. I found they had made most satisfactory arrangements on my behalf. These enabled me to leave the station without a finger being raised by immigration or customs.

I had arrived in a ramshackle town with facilities unequal to the invasion of journalists that was taking place. Most of them were quartered in great discomfort at the Imperial Hotel. Always fearful of missing a story, reporters on a major assignment often stick close together, so they packed into this relatively small hotel, close to the radio station from which everyone's copy had to be sent, sleeping four to a room but secure in the knowledge that they could keep an eye on each other. This was the hotel which Evelyn Waugh called the Splendide in his account of the war, *Waugh in Abyssinia*, and from which he drew his portrait of the Hotel Liberty, Jacksonburg, in *Scoop*.

My friend Stuart Emeny, Evelyn Waugh and a few others had made altogether better arrangements in a nearby pension, run by a German couple, Mr and Mrs Heft. It was close to the

Imperial and the radio station, was on a single floor with a
balcony running round it and had ten or a dozen rooms. It
was, as Waugh put it, humbler than the Imperial but very
much more hospitable. On the night of my arrival it was full,
so Salmon had arranged for me to spend a single night at the
Hotel D'Europe, which was comfortable enough with a bathroom to every room but five miles from the centre of Addis,
which rendered it unsuitable for a journalist. We dined
together and, next day, which was a public holiday, I had
ample time to shift my stuff to the Deutsches Haus. Its surroundings were unimpressive. Immediately opposite was a
tannery which often smelt offensively; nearby were the homes
of local prostitutes. But, as Waugh was to write later, 'though
the surroundings were forbidding, the hospitality inside the
gates (which were kept by a grizzled warrior armed with a
seven-foot spear) was delightful'.

His description of the Hefts first appeared in the pro-Italian
and controversial *Waugh in Abyssinia* (1936), now out of
print but reprised in his much-shortened version, *A War in
1935*, which appeared with four other accounts of his travels
in *When the Going Was Good* (1946). Since they were to be
my hosts for the next three months, I reproduce part of
Waugh's very accurate sketch:

> Mrs Heft was one of the Germans who had drifted
> to Abyssinia from Tanganyika when it was
> confiscated by the British Government. There were
> a large number of her compatriots in the town,
> mostly in very poor circumstances, employed as

mechanics or in petty trade. The Deutsches Haus was their rendezvous where they played cards and occasionally dined. The Hefts could never quite get used to the disregard of small economies or the modest appetites of her new boarders. Many of our demands seemed to her painfully complex. 'The journalists pay well,' she confided. 'But they are very difficult. Some want coffee in the morning and some want tea, and they expect it always to be hot.' But she worked untiringly in our service.

She was a housewife of formidable efficiency. Daily from dawn until noon a miniature market was held on the steps of the dining-room. Half a dozen native hawkers squatted patiently, displaying meat, eggs, and vegetables. Every half-hour she or Mr Heft would emerge, disparage the goods, ask the price, and, in sham rage, tell the salesmen to be off. Eventually, when it was time to start cooking luncheon, she made her purchases . . .

There were two geese in the yard who attacked all comers. Mr Heft was always promising to kill them, but they were still alive when I left the country. There was also a pig, which he did kill, from which Mrs Heft made a magnificent abundance of sausages and *pâtés*. The food, for Addis, was excellent. Mr Heft hovered over the tables at meal times watching all we ate. 'No like?' he would say, in genuine distress, if anyone refused a course. 'Make you eggies, yes?'

The Hefts' bedroom opened from the dining-room, and it was there that everything of value in the house was kept. If one wanted change for a hundred-thaler note, an aspirin, a clean towel, a slice of sausage, a bottle of Chianti, the wireless bulletin, a spare part for a car, a pack of cards, one's washing or one's weekly bill, Mrs Heft dived under the bed and produced it.

I had not been in Addis Ababa many hours before thanking my lucky stars that my boat had sailed from Marseilles a fortnight after the ship in which Evelyn Waugh, Stuart Emeny and others had travelled. One of their companions, who joined the ship at Port Said, had been a Mr F. W. Rickett. To his credit, Waugh had spotted something fishy about him but sent only a leisurely letter of inquiry from the Red Sea to his friend in England, Penelope (wife of John) Betjeman: 'Can you find out for me anything about a man who should be a neighbour of yours, named Rickett? He says he is master of the *Craven* & lives near Newbury. I want particularly to know how he earns his living, whether he is in the British secret service and whether he is connected with Vickers or Imperial Chemicals . . . Reply poste restante Addis Ababa.'

According to Waugh's own account, Rickett talked about a 'mission' and when questioned by Stuart Emeny about it, hinted that he was bringing Coptic funds to the Abuna, the patriarch of the Abyssinian Orthodox Church. He spoke about his pack of hounds in the Midlands and, on receiving lengthy cables in code, declared they came from his huntsman.

'He says the prospects for cubbin' are excellent.' Waugh put him down as one of the many arms salesmen who were heading for Addis Ababa. Because the Imperial Hotel was full, Rickett failed to get the suite he had ordered there and had to accept humbler accommodation with Waugh and Emeny at the Deutsches Haus.

Rickett then vanished into the shadows, and no more was heard of him until Saturday 31 August when a huge splash in *The Daily Telegraph* announced to the world, 'Abyssinia's £10,000,000 Deal with British & U.S. Interests.' This was how Sir Percival Phillips, *Daily Telegraph* Special Correspondent in Addis Ababa, began this revelation which, regardless of cable costs, ran to something like 3,000 words:

> A few strokes of an ordinary black fountain-pen this morning performed one of the most momentous and far-reaching acts in the history of Ethiopia, bringing her out from the Middle Ages and setting her fairly on the road of the twentieth century.
>
> The instrument of this transformation is a Convention conferring on Mr F. W. Rickett, an envoy of the African Exploitation and Development Corporation, the sole rights to oil, minerals and other natural resources over half the Empire for a period of 75 years.
>
> It enables an intensive development by British and American capital, on a scale far beyond the wildest dreams of foreign applicants for concessions in the past. Many have tried repeatedly to break

down the barriers of Ethiopian conservatism, and have as repeatedly failed.

As *The Daily Telegraph* reported in a second splash on the following Monday, 'the news caused a stir all over the world'. Nowhere did it cause a bigger stir than in the offices of those newspapers which had expensively sent correspondents to Abyssinia but had failed to land the story. After completing the agreement, Rickett appears to have decided that his clients' interests would be best served if he revealed its contents exclusively to two major correspondents close at hand: Jim Mills, who was in Addis Ababa for the Associated Press of America, and Phillips of *The Daily Telegraph*. This meant that every other news agency and newspaper in the world was scuppered.

Waugh could hardly have known what a particularly bitter blow this would be to the *Daily Mail*, which had employed Phillips as its special correspondent from 1922 until the previous year, when Phillips is said to have quarrelled with Lord Rothermere, proprietor of the *Daily Mail*, and defected to the *Telegraph*. Phillips was one of the half-dozen newspaper correspondents who had received knighthoods for their reporting of the First World War. After working in America, he joined the *Daily Express* in 1901 and remained with them until 1922 when he joined the *Mail*. He was an experienced correspondent and a smart operator.

And where was Waugh during this drama? Some 200 miles away in Harar and Jijiga. Having arrived in Addis Ababa in mid-August and decided that it offered none of the news for which the *Daily Mail* was hungering, he had in all good faith gone east with his friend Patrick Balfour (later Lord Kinross), the *Evening Standard* correspondent, to explore what stories those regions could provide. He was attracted by Harar, an ancient Arab city which he had first seen during his visit to Abyssinia in 1930. It had come down in the world since then, but still offered attractions. Many thought that Italy would start the war in that area. With that in mind, Waugh and Balfour sensibly decided to spend a few days down there looking around. It turned out to be a disastrous decision. They were still there at the end of August when the Phillips splash appeared. An urgent telegram from the *Daily Mail*, 'What do you know Anglo-American oil concession?' left Waugh baffled. He knew nothing about it, and while in Harar had no means of finding out.

It was four days before Waugh could get back to Addis Ababa, and by then the Rickett story was dead. The agreement had of course been seen by the Emperor as a way of enlisting American interests and perhaps support. Cordell Hull at America's State Department, Eden of Great Britain and Laval of France saw that quickly – and the dangers it entailed. The deal was squashed, leaving behind it a trail of urgent and sometimes angry cables to the correspondents in Addis Ababa.

The angriest of all were directed by the *Daily Mail* at Evelyn Waugh and were still arriving when I took my first breakfast at the Deutsches Haus. Waugh affected to treat them lightly and would occasionally use one of them as a spill for his after-breakfast cigar. But they had certain consequences, which is why such a small episode in the history of the twentieth century is worth recalling. They signalled the end of Waugh's working arrangements with the *Mail* and provoked in him a feeling of resentment against his more professional colleagues in journalism which, I have always believed, provided the impetus for his novel *Scoop*. We see evidence of this in a letter he wrote to Katharine Asquith from Addis Ababa about the time of my arrival. Katharine Asquith, daughter-in-law of the former prime minister, had become Lady Horner. A Catholic convert, she was fifty in 1935 and a considerable figure in society. Waugh was at first nervous of her, but they became and [remained close friends until his death. The relevant passage in his letter to her reads:

> *The journalists are lousy competitive hysterical lying* [sic]. *It makes me unhappy to be one of them but that will soon be OK as the* Daily Mail *don't like the messages I send them and I don't like what they send me but I don't want to chuck them on account of honour because they have given me this holiday at great expense and would be left in the soup if I stopped sending them even my unsatisfactory messages; they don't want to sack me for identical reasons. So it is deadlock and we telegraph abuse at 4 and something a word.*

The telegram rate was not, in fact, '4 and something' but two shillings and sixpence a word at urgent rates, which every correspondent felt compelled to use and so became the going rate. Moreover, Waugh did try to cancel his contract with the *Mail* and wrote to his agent A. D. Peters telling him so. 'I am sending in my resignation to the mail [*sic*]. It wasn't possible for me to work with them as they have all the wrong ideas.' This led to impasse. Waugh did not wish to leave Abyssinia because he still had his book contracts to fulfil for *Waugh in Abyssinia*, which attracted modest public attention when it was published, and *Scoop*, which took him longer but eventually appeared in 1938 and proved a huge success. The *Daily Mail* sent a replacement, W. F. 'Binks' Hartin, a first-class reporter whom I had met a couple of years earlier while we were working for our newspapers on a murder mystery, the Brighton trunk crime.

But the Abyssinians reckoned that one man from the *Mail* at any one time was enough. The *Mail* was not as pro-Italian as Waugh himself but was some way from being pro-Abyssinian. So Waugh remained inside the country and 'Binks' Hartin languished at Djibouti, where he contracted dysentery. Happily he recovered, and four years later we became riflemen together in the Queen's Westminsters (KRRC).

That was roughly how I found things on arrival at the Deutsches Haus. At the age of thirty-two, Waugh was an experienced traveller, particularly in Africa, and a successful novelist. *Decline and Fall* (1928) and *Vile Bodies* (1930) had at least startled people into paying attention to what he wrote. *Black Mischief* (1932), written after his experiences at the coronation of the Emperor Haile Selassie in 1930, was a topical comedy written about a university-educated black trying to drag his savage country into the modern world. It also introduced his readers to Basil Seal, who was to be the central figure in *Put Out More Flags* (1942). Waugh's study of Edmund Campion, written partly to establish his religious credentials in the eyes of the Roman Catholic hierarchy, partly as a gift to the rebuilding of Oxford's Campion Hall, had also won him the prestigious Hawthornden Prize. What had signalled his arrival in the front rank of contemporary novelists was *Handful of Dust*, which appeared in 1934. Not everybody enjoyed it, for its portrait of human nature is dark, but many admired it.

So, regardless of how relations stood with the *Daily Mail*, Waugh's reputation as a writer was established. In the world of today he could well have been rich, but in the mid-1930s earning enough to keep pace with the standard of living he chose for himself was a serious business. For this assignment he had sought through his agent roughly the sort of deal they had secured for the Emperor's coronation in 1930.

For the coronation, *The Times* had hired him as their special correspondent, and a very good choice it had turned out to be. As was the custom in those days, Waugh's name did not appear over the copy, but the style of the pieces was unmistakably his. While we were together in Addis Ababa, Waugh boasted to me that he had posted his account of the coronation to *The Times*, a method of despatch which had caused them displeasure. It might well have done, as the mail would have taken three weeks or more. It turned out to be a typical Waugh invention, perhaps devised to impress me with his disdain for journalism. Called on by a publisher some years later to write the introduction to a new edition of Waugh's *Black Mischief*, I sought the help of *The Times* library. We turned up his copy. True, some of it had been delayed – due to abysmal conditions at the Addis Ababa radio station – but it was all there and it read well. The other two prongs of a Waugh travel deal, as he explained to me, were a serious book and a novel. After the coronation, he had written a short but serious account of the event which appeared in *Remote People*. *Black Mischief* had followed two years later.

It followed that on all such assignments Waugh's concentration was divided and not exclusively devoted to the interests of his newspaper. Note the wealth of detail with which he was able to describe the Heft regime at the Deutsches Haus, which would have been of no interest at all to the *Daily Mail*. Indeed, he affected to despise those of us who made the newspaper our sole concern. He mocked my friend Stuart Emeny's devotion to duty on behalf of the *News Chronicle*. Contemptuously referring to him as 'a reporter from a Radical newspaper' or 'the Radical', Waugh observed of him, 'I did not know it was possible for a human being to identify himself so precisely with the interests of his employers.' It is in fact how most good reporters go about their work and is, after all, the only string to their bow. Newspapers are competitive, demanding and sometimes totally unreasonable, and so were unsuitable for someone of Waugh's temperament. In Abyssinia I worked closely with Stuart Emeny and learned a lot from him. Waugh found our remorseless hunt for non-existent news stories faintly contemptible, but we all had to live together, so for the most part he passed it off as good-humoured banter.

One needs to remember also, though none of us in Addis Ababa was remotely aware of it at the time, that Waugh was preoccupied with his private life. His marriage to Evelyn Gardner in 1928 had ended in divorce a year later. In September 1930 he had been received into the Roman Catholic Church. Early in 1935 he fell in love with Laura Herbert, whose mother, Lady Herbert, had her doubts about Waugh and he could make no decisive move until Rome had agreed to the annulment of his marriage. This agreement did not come through until July 1936. He needed the proceeds of *Scoop* to pay for his marriage to Laura in April 1937 and their new home. These events may partly explain his sometimes erratic behaviour in Addis Ababa during 1935.

I have often been asked what I made of Waugh. He had a weakness for well-connected people, but unlike a lot of so-called snobs, he was adept at conversing with people of small importance, though often baffling them with his brand of wit. He paid close attention to what they said to him, which is why dialogue in his novels rings so true. Some, for example, think that his portrait of the young officer Hooper in *Brideshead Revisited* is odious and unfair. But it is a true portrait of a type we all encountered in the army as it expanded during the Second World War.

When in Waugh's company, I always felt secretly relieved that I had been to a good public school, although Waugh did not think highly of Harrow; it was where poor Giles of *Decline and Fall* had been educated. None of us quite measured up to the sort of company he liked to keep back at home. He openly mocked the American correspondents and would gleefully mimic their accents. As *Scoop* makes abundantly clear, he especially looked down on reporters and photographers sent to Abyssinia by the popular press. On the other hand, Waugh was a more experienced traveller than any of us. He knew Africa; he had been in Abyssinia five years earlier. So, literary talent apart, he established a sort of leadership which drew respect. If you got bitten by a scorpion, he was the man you were most likely to consult. In his heart, he knew he had to take the world as he found it, not as it was in one of his London clubs. In the drab world of Addis Ababa, that made him, at least to some of us, a good companion.

A lifetime in journalism has taught me that people have to be judged in the context of their times, and that is what newspapers and television so often overlook. In those early days of Evelyn Waugh's success there were many fashionable people happy to entertain and lionize authors in the public eye, particularly if they were 'amusing', which to some Waugh was. He did not have to seek their society; they would seek him out for house parties, cocktail parties, any social gathering. In the early 1930s I was sometimes sent as a reporter to one of the literary lunches held by the late Christina Foyle of Foyle's Bookshop. Authors in the news had the sort of following there that pop stars now attract from the young.

Waugh also had much in common with my young friends whom the *Morning Post* was recruiting from Oxford and Cambridge at the time I joined the newspaper. We went to parties most evenings, frequented smart nightclubs, drank too much and sometimes behaved badly, while automatically asserting what we supposed to be our social superiority. As he grew older, Waugh became more eccentric. In the mid-1930s his talent was outstanding but his behaviour not all out of line with that of many contemporaries.

Three

Waugh was right about one thing: hard news in Addis was hard to find. My first story from Abyssinia, which for want of anything better the *Morning Post* made the splash, was about the weather.

'Despite confident predictions to the contrary,' I cabled, 'torrential rains, bringing as much as one and a half inches in one day, continue to sweep the upland plateaux and mountains the whole length of Abyssinia. It is expected they will continue for exactly another fortnight – until September 27th.' Those familiar with the north of the country declared that the rain ruled out any advance by the Italians for at least a month. Some forty-five inches had fallen on Abyssinia that season – roughly the same amount as fell on parts of England during the wet weather of 2001.

It made a start, but there were limits to how far one could make the weather interesting. By this time there were seventy-five journalists in Addis Ababa and another thirty were reported to be on their way. They came from every part of the world. Some fourteen had arrived on my train, only three of whom spoke English. Less than half of them, I told our foreign editor, were filing regularly. Strange though it seems these days, only one of the seventy-five was engaged in filming. He was a swaggering, noisy man called Lawrence Stallings, famed author of two popular American films about the First World War, *What Price Glory?* and *The Big Parade*. He was in charge of the lavishly equipped Fox Movietone outfit. Waugh thought him ridiculous. I found him fascinating, with his ranch clothes and big voice, embodying all that one imagined a Hollywood mogul to be.

An official press bureau had been established which in truly bureaucratic fashion sought to become the sole channel of news. It dished out statements – if there were any – twice a day and directed that no information be sought through any other Abyssinian channel. Even an interview with the Emperor, as I explained to my foreign editor, had to be conducted on the lines of an income tax return. One entered a dozen or more questions in writing and received the answers within about three days, apparently dictated by the Emperor. The answers everyone received to their differing questions appeared to be very much the same. There was no censorship as such, but there was nothing for a censor to do.

Looking at it now from a more relaxed viewpoint, one can see how difficult it was for them. There had long been petty fighting within Abyssinia which had been of no interest to foreign newspapers. The possibility of war with another country was outside the country's recent experience and handling the international press in such a situation was something for which the government was wholly unprepared. In any case, the initiative lay with the Italians; Abyssinian officials had no more idea of what Italy was planning than we had. So we suffered a news vacuum, while our newspapers, aware of what it cost to keep a special correspondent in Addis Ababa, waited anxiously for a return on their money. I had nothing to complain about. The *Morning Post* never pestered me and occasionally sent messages of encouragement.

There were of course other sources to be tapped in Addis Ababa. The British legation under Sir Sidney Barton was a friendly place. The first secretary invited me to lunch and I came to know the military attaché. One or two of us were invited to dine with the French minister. Government departments lived in lowly buildings, some of them no better than mud huts, but the legations, most of them tucked away in the hills well outside the capital, were much grander. Our own (now an embassy) occupies, or did in the mid-1990s when I last stayed there, some ninety acres of land. It was a relatively small but beautifully proportioned single-storey building, covered with creeper and rather homely. Set in so much land, it left you with the impression of a small English country house with a park, its acreage exceeding that enjoyed by any of our grander embassies in the world. It had been a gift to the British from the Emperor Menelik II.

Our social life was unexpectedly busy. Lady Barton gave a cocktail party at the legation and one evening we had a formal reception at the palace and were afforded brief individual audiences with the Emperor. What can you do on such occasions except exchange minor pleasantries? 'I am glad you have come to our land.' 'I am glad to be in your land, Emperor.' Nowhere in the world have I ever sought audience with the top man or woman; the ritual consumes the best part of a day and there is very little to show for it in the newspaper. Stuart Emeny and I dined with an influential American couple, the Colsons. He was financial adviser to the Emperor and useful.

When nobody invited us out, there were two cinemas in the town, each of which held about 150 people. One was Le Perroquet run by Madame Idot, the other was Mon Cine, run by Madame Moriatis. Both of them had bars and served as nightclubs. The films were old but good. Once a week we went to the comfortable Hotel D'Europe for baths. I was told the Emperor went there too; hot water was scarce in Addis Ababa. The Emperor had in fact abandoned the old Gibbi, the old palace of Menelik's time, which remained Imperial headquarters and was used for court functions but not as a residence. Waugh likened the new Gibbi to the 'villa of a retired Midland magnate'. It had been fashionably but not cosily furnished by Waring and Gillow, the London store. On the evening he gave a banquet to the foreign press the footmen wore European dress and the lights went out five times. It was, I wrote to my mother, 'a terrific meal of fairly European quality, with rather foul wines of Ethiopian quality'. The exception was the liqueur we were offered, which was *tej*, a delicious honey-based drink of considerable authority. The Emperor's *tej* was very fine indeed. After a glass or two, nobody wanted to go to bed, so after we left the new palace the party continued elsewhere. Astonishingly, I attended the banquet in white tie and tails. It was the dress called for on such an occasion, but not many were in possession of it. *Autres temps, autres mœurs*, but what war correspondent today would dream of travelling with full evening dress? I cannot remember what Evelyn Waugh, a light packer, wore on this occasion, but it could hardly have been less than black tie.

What made life expensive was travelling to these entertainments, some of them a long way outside the capital. Theoretically, we should have been doing it on horseback; that was the reason for buying riding breeches (for winter and summer wear) from Austin Reed. But, as I explained in a letter to my foreign editor, 'riding is out of the question, partly because of the motor traffic on bad roads and partly because the rainy season makes it extremely dangerous.' Addis Ababa in 1935 was still a capital where the inhabitants felt free to drive flocks of goats or sheep along the unmade roads, and most people travelled on donkeys or mules. It was the pace of life. Into this pastoral tranquillity the motor car suddenly intruded. Taxis hired by journalists were driven impatiently round the straggling city. A taxi I hired in my first days there crashed into a group of Abyssinians and seriously injured two of them. The police arrived and apologized to the white man for the inconvenience caused.

Enough of that, I thought, and rented by the week a relatively modern Chrysler with a smart and intelligent Sikh driver. Taxis, I explained to my foreign editor, were expensive and unsuitable because they often required one to travel with other reporters. Hiring my Chrysler, at twelve thalers a day (£7 a week), which included the driver's wages and petrol, was cheaper than the promiscuous hire of taxis which could amount to twenty thalers a day. A horse, I pointed out, would cost about twenty pounds for starters with weekly expenses of at least eight pounds for stabling, food and groom. Moreover, in competing with journalists with fast cars one would be handicapped. In 1935, seven pounds a week was a good income; with an annual salary of £360, you could buy a house. Nonetheless, the *Morning Post* accepted my reasoning.

Stuart Emeny and I agreed, however, that on the outbreak of war we would not be able to travel far round the country in a Chrysler as there were no roads, only rough tracks. Evelyn Waugh concurred. So we instituted a small private riding school. Early in the morning, the three of us would set forth on locally hired horses. Waugh had learned his riding in a hard school and proved an excellent instructor. He rode behind us, shouting instructions and saying rude things about the expanse of daylight he saw between our seats and the saddle. I slowly acclimatized myself to life in the saddle, and this was as well because our friends at the British legation suddenly proposed a Sunday morning ride and picnic.

It involved riding to the legation which was some miles from Deutsches Haus, joining up with a small legation party on horseback and then riding for three hours to a suitable venue for lunch. I found it anxious work. Everyone seemed on better terms with their horse than I was. Mine had been the property of an official at the Italian legation, was full of oats, badly short of exercise and so difficult to handle. I remember nothing about the lunch, except that it began with brimming glasses of gin and vermouth and ended with a fruit salad. Egged on by Waugh, the military attaché poured a generous portion of gin into the fruit. Nobody spotted this and most of the company thought it delicious. But when we mounted and turned for home, the horses may well have felt the need to take charge of some of their riders. The risk of falling off had greatly increased but fear of falling off had diminished. The secretary to the legation, a Mr Roberts, was so tight that he fell off his horse while it was stationary. We all got safely home.

Waugh's relations with the British legation were complicated. Sir Sidney Barton had been our minister in Addis Ababa at the time of the Emperor's coronation in 1930 and was still there in 1935. He had a daughter called Esme. In his novel *Black Mischief*, written after his experiences in Addis Ababa in 1930, Waugh's British envoy in Azania is Sir Samson Courteney. His daughter Prudence has an affair with Basil Seal and in a macabre ending to the novel is eaten by cannibals. Waugh always insisted, I think with truth, that the Courteneys had no connection in his mind with the Bartons. People writing about Waugh have often sought to identify his characters with real people. Occasionally they are right but more often they are wrong because, as I explain later when dealing with his novel *Scoop*, Waugh like most good novelists drew on more than one person for each of his characters. He drew on me for my excessive baggage – and perhaps for my naivety – but I am no more the William Boot of *Scoop* than I am the Man in the Moon.

The Bartons, however, could be forgiven for seeing Waugh's portrait of a British envoy as drawn from his recollection of the British legation in Addis Ababa in 1930. Esme took offence, and in one of Addis Ababa's two nightclubs, where Waugh and I were drinking his revolting mixture of brandy and crème de menthe, she appeared one evening and tossed a glass of wine into his face. I remember feeling rather embarrassed at the attention the incident aroused, but Waugh laughed it off. 'How frightfully funny,' he said, wiping his face. However, in the British foreign service, ambassadors and ministers have to subdue personal likes and dislikes; Sir Sidney treated us all, including Waugh, with an even hand and so did his staff.

All our small purchases and the payment of servants were transacted in the Maria Theresa thaler, a handsome coin roughly the size of the British five-shilling piece. Today it has been replaced by paper money and become a collector's item but a century earlier it had been the coin of the Arab trader almost everywhere. In 1935 it survived only in Arabia and Abyssinia. Still being minted in Vienna from the 1780 die, it was singular in that its silver content was worth more than its exchange value. This led to dubious transactions. I reported from Addis Ababa that despite an embargo on its export the thaler was leaving the country at the rate of half a million monthly. It was worth eighty-four rupees in Addis Ababa, ninety-seven rupees in Dire Dawa and 132 in Djibouti. One grew accustomed to humping these coins round in a canvas bag. We used them at our occasional poker table. Mercifully all our cables sent from the radio station were 'press collect' and paid for at the other end, or we would have needed a handcart to carry our cash.

With war looming, most commerce in Abyssinia was in a wretched state. The export trade in hides, coffee and butter had vanished and as a result government tax revenues had collapsed. A small minority by contrast was making enormous profits out of the emergency, as often happens in war. The hotel trade was prospering, as were the taxi proprietors who had invested in vast American motor cars. The word was that, because of the altitude, walking was dangerous. At twenty-two, I hardly noticed it, except for occasional breathlessness, but a number of correspondents felt downright ill. I noticed that one or two of the Europeans permanently stationed in Addis had the bad colour that one associates with heart problems. Sir Percival Phillips of *The Daily Telegraph*, who was fifty-eight, told me he found the altitude troublesome and eventually had to leave Addis altogether. When I went back there in 2001 at the age of eighty-seven for the burial of the Emperor's remains, I did notice the altitude and found it desirable to walk slowly and climb stairs very slowly.

For all journalists the most trying feature of life in Addis Ababa was not the altitude but isolation from the outside world. Wireless lacked the range it has today. The legations had some idea of what was going on, but were an unreliable way of keeping in touch with events. I suggested to the *Morning Post* that the foreign room cabled me briefly on anything important which bore on the situation in Abyssinia. 'So much,' I wrote to them 'now depends on rumour. Tonight (September 12) we are informed that general mobilisation has been ordered in Italy. Much of this stuff should of course be followed up here.' Being cut off from the world made news-gathering in Addis Ababa much more difficult. I noticed also that correspondents who were kept informed by their offices of what was going on in the world always had items of news to trade with their friends in the legations and elsewhere. Embassies are there partly to gather intelligence, so the journalist who can tell them something they do not already know is always welcome and that is as true today as it was then.

Sir Percival Phillips held a strong advantage here. He and Jim Mills of Associated Press of America pooled their local and special correspondents and other helpers. This gave them a staff of six competent journalists and one or two assistants whom they directed from a room in the Imperial Hotel. They also received daily cables from their offices in Geneva and elsewhere which made them valuable to the Abyssinian authorities. With a really juicy piece of news from the outside world, the correspondent might expect to be taken straight to the Emperor or the foreign minister and perhaps granted an interview. All this I pointed out rather plaintively to the *Morning Post*. 'With a staff of six men to run round all day collecting news, and being in a position to sit quietly in his hotel and write up the results, Sir Percival has most of us beat,' I told my foreign editor. In fact, after his great scoop on the Rickett affair, Phillips could afford to take things easy. It was the best exclusive story of the war.

Twice a week we paraded at the railway station to see the train from the coast pull in. After the Rickett episode, we were like cats watching a hole down which a mouse has once been seen to disappear. I cannot remember anyone of note catching my eye, but the more I saw of that railway, the more it struck me as essential and vulnerable. Everything worth having had to come up on that line; apart from passengers there was also heavy freight traffic. Stuart Emeny and I made enquiries and filed a story which the *Morning Post* made the splash. The Abyssinian government, we reported, was preparing plans for the railway's defence. There would be armed guards on bridges and troops stationed at strategic points along the line. To assist this defence, machine guns were urgently needed.

We talked to the railway authorities, who admitted privately that effective defence of the line was impossible. Stretches of it were in wild country where the locals occasionally cut the telephone wires to steal the copper. There was a 150-metre bridge at Awas high above the river which, if bombed, would be difficult to replace quickly. Against this, we reasoned, the Italians would see the potential value of the railway line to themselves. They were wonderful road builders but it would have taken them a long time to build a road capable of bearing the traffic the railway carried. It had fifty locomotives and a thousand carriages and wagons.

Late on the night of 22 September, the Italians delivered their final terms to the League of Geneva. Their demand for the cession of Abyssinian territory linking Eritrea and Italian Somaliland would have had the effect of bringing Addis Ababa on to Italian soil. They also sought the total disarmament of Abyssinia and stipulated that any police or other forces should be placed completely under Italian control. As the *Morning Post* correspondent in Geneva aptly observed, 'comment on this counter offer is superfluous.' Italy had signalled her determination to go to war.

With this came news, which I reported from Addis, of

permission being granted for the departure of all Italy's consuls stationed in different parts of the country and speculation increased on the most likely Italian plan of attack. The Abyssinian authorities said they expected the main thrust to come from Assab through Aussa in the north and through the Ogaden in the south. I dispatched all this, while warning *Morning Post* readers that such statements might be coloured by a desire to set Italian minds working along certain lines. Of greater relevance was Abyssinian anxiety about the integrity of some of the chiefs. Part of the Italian strategy was to sound them out and, if possible, bribe them. We were not in a united country, far from it. Abyssinia was a fractious kingdom, seamed with treachery. A significant threat to the Emperor throughout the war was the disloyalty of those who owed him allegiance.

In her darkest hour, I reported from Addis Ababa on 26 September 1935, Abyssinia was preparing for its greatest feast. This was the Feast of the Masqal, which was held on the same day every year, 27 September, to mark the end of the rains. Drums were calling men to arms elsewhere in Abyssinia, but in Addis Ababa there would be feasting and drinking in celebrations which, I fancifully suggested, combined the Lord Mayor's Show, an eisteddfod and Trooping the Colour. The Masqal was a tall post with a bunch of flowers at the top of it. Up to midday, when the ceremony was due to start, the weather had been fine and sunny, but soon after that it began to rain, which seemed a bad omen. As the Emperor with an escort of the Imperial Guard drove up, torrential rain swept across the scene. Thunder rumbled and soon the square was flooded. The crowd was soaked and water burst through the roof of our stand.

I watched the Emperor sitting on his throne gazing with an expressionless face upon the sodden scene. By 2.45 the storm had reached its height. Hail followed and beat on what was left of the corrugated iron above our heads like thunder. At 3.15, during a brief respite, the Abuna emerged to do his duty and walked round the Masqal. The Emperor and his son, the Duke of Harar, followed him. Then the parade began.

It was a curious mixture of disciplined troops and shapeless feudal levies. War chiefs in dripping fur danced past the throne boasting of their past and future achievements. There followed the new army of volunteers; Waugh, as he expressed it in *Waugh in Abyssinia*, thought it an unhappy compromise. 'There was nothing at all ridiculous about the totally undisciplined little companies, who cheered and stumbled and chattered and jostled round their chiefs; but the volunteers, laboriously attempting to keep step, with their caps at odd angles, and expressions on their faces of extreme self-consciousness, made a very silly show.'

Hundreds followed in procession before the throne – boasting, singing and casting flower-decked sticks at the foot of the maypole. Liberated slaves passed, celebrating their freedom, then more chiefs on splendidly caparisoned horses, accompanied by thousands of retainers. Then, in contrast, came the modern army, and the dignified march of the Imperial Guard. 'The noise of the distant tribes died,' I wrote. 'There was only the sound of the soft pad and splash of naked feet across the flooded square.'

Even allowing for the rain, I thought it a forlorn show; although it seemed to buck the Abyssinians up no end, I sensed that these colourful warriors would be no match for a modern European army. One had no inkling of the new weapons of war which Germany and Italy were then producing, some of which were to demonstrate their power in the Spanish Civil War which broke out a year later. The afternoon would have been even more dispiriting had we known more of what modern war would entail.

The afternoon led to our first casualty. William Barber of the *Chicago Tribune* had contracted malaria in Harar a month earlier. He got soaking wet at the Masqal ceremony and caught a chill which turned to pneumonia. At that point he developed blackwater fever and died of kidney failure. The Emperor was distressed. On hearing of Barber's illness, he offered to allow Barber's wife to fly direct from London to Addis Ababa, which was normally impossible. Barber died in hospital the day that permission was granted. We were all shocked – except Waugh. Barber was an American correspondent and Waugh declined to take any American correspondent, alive or dead, seriously. 'Poor Barber . . .' he would intone in a mock solemn voice.

His badly typewritten letter to Laura Herbert about the event reveals his mood:

> We had our first death too and a latter day
> Adventist funeral with extempore prayers by an
> American minister. 'O god please help us the late
> departed's sorrowing colleagues and do the best

thou canst o god to cheer up his poor wife I
know it is hard for you o god but have a try. O
god thou has appointed three score years and ten
as man's allotted span but O god statistics go to
prove that comparatively few ever attain that age'
and so on well that was fun but now things have
settled down again . . .

But Barber had a good funeral which we all attended. The service was conducted by the American mission and took place in a small graveyard in the surrounding hills. Most of the legations were represented and there was a cortège of forty cars from the hospital to the church. The coffin was impressively wrapped in the Stars and Stripes.

On health grounds the rest of us had little to worry about; flying ants and flies, with the occasional flea or mosquito were the main pests, and at that altitude the mosquitoes were said to be harmless. Black ants were painful but not harmful. Water was pure, though not tasty. I gave salads and milk a miss, but otherwise ate everything set in front of me.

On 28 September, without knowing what was going on anywhere else in the world, we somehow sensed that war was only a few days off. Abyssinia was on the brink of general mobilization. The Emperor sent a telegram to the president of the Council of the League of Nations which read:

Firmly devoted to peace, we shall continue to
collaborate with the Council in the hope of a
peaceful solution under the Covenant.

*But we must draw the most serious attention
of the Council to the increasing gravity of the
menace of Italian aggression by the continual
dispatch of reinforcements and other
preparations, despite our pacific attitude.*

*We must ask the Council to take as soon as
possible all measures of precaution against Italian
aggression, for the time has come when we would
be failing in our duty if we delay longer the
general mobilisation we have in mind.*

That telegram was sent on the advice of the Abyssinian
delegation in Geneva, who sensed the game was up. In what
had largely become a game of bluff, the League of Nations of
those years lacked the chips to see Mussolini off. So, as I
reported at the time, Ethiopia would mobilize, but remain
determined that the first act of aggression should come from
the other side. Meanwhile, perversely and unseasonably, the
rain continued to fall in torrents.

At this point the white population in Abyssinia, most of it in
Addis Ababa, had a last chance to decide where they wanted to
be in the war. There were remarkably few departures. At least
90 per cent, I reported, decided to see it through. The British
legation had the care of about 1,200 subjects in the country.
The French had about 400, the Americans barely 100, half of
them in the capital and half in the interior. There were 300
Germans and thirty Austrians. Not altogether surprisingly, only
twenty Italians remained, including the six consuls who had
been called in and five at the legation. The Greek population

was big, with 1,500 in Addis Ababa and 4,000 elsewhere.

Among the journalists boredom prevailed. Constantly badgered by their offices for news, which they could not find, they grew morose and began to deliver protests. The Foreign Press Association, which occasionally met at the Splendide Hotel, sought to secure some sort of leverage over the Abyssinian government but suffered too many internal quarrels to be effective. The American and the French were never on the same wavelength. Journalists accusing each other of cheating made little impact on Abyssinian press bureau officials, so when it came to serious questions, such as when we would be permitted to visit the war fronts, the FPA was simply ignored and eventually dissolved.

Waugh satirized the sort of squabbling that went on in *Scoop*:

> The voice of the secretary could occasionally be heard above the chatter . . . held at the Hotel Liberty . . . Sir Jocelyn Hitchcock in the chair . . . resolution . . . unanimously passed . . . protest in the most emphatic manner against . . . Ishmaelite government . . . militates against professional activities . . .
>
> At this stage one half of the audience – those nearest William – were distracted from the proceedings by an altercation, unconnected with the business in hand, between two rival photographers.
>
> 'Did you call me a scab?'
>
> 'I did not, but I will.'
>
> 'You will?'

'Sure, you're a scab. Now what?'
'Call me a scab outside.'
'I call you a scab here.'
'Say that outside and see what you get.'
Cries of 'Shame' and 'Aw, pipe down.'

True to life.

Waugh had his own approach to relieving the tedium. He livened up our quarters by purchasing a baboon, which slept in his room at the Deutsches Haus but spent its days chained up and hunched at the entrance – 'a petulant and humourless baboon', Waugh called it and named it 'B'abunah', after the local archbishop with whom he was acquainted. Later he declared it was showing signs of affection. But it was a noisy brute and struck me as of uncertain temperament; I gave it a wide berth. The Reuters correspondent, Collins, who had a house to himself, bought four monkeys. They were a cheap buy, costing only a few pennies each.

Knickerbocker had started a small poker school which Waugh and I sometimes joined. We played for modest quantities of silver thalers. The highlight of these evenings was Knickerbocker's cooking of corned beef hash, of which he was fond and persuaded us to enjoy. It was at one of these evenings that Knickerbocker and Waugh fell out and engaged in a bout of fisticuffs.

They were discussing novelists and Knickerbocker remarked that he thought Waugh came second only to Aldous Huxley (*Antic Hay*, 1923, *Brave New World*, 1932). Waugh chose to take offence at this observation and declared that the matter could only be settled by a knockabout. They stepped outside the French windows of Knickerbocker's rather grand apartment on the ground floor of the hotel and shaped up on the patch of green outside. I held Knickerbocker's spectacles. After a brief flurry in which no serious blows were exchanged, honour was satisfied. Most people would conclude that alcohol had played some part in this, but to the best of my recollection it had been rather a sober evening. It was more attributable, I think, to Waugh's weakness for theatricality, and perhaps owed something to the altitude which had the effect of shortening some people's tempers.

Though constantly derided by Waugh, Knickerbocker had made his way to the top of the Hearst news organization by being an enterprising correspondent. He was generous to me and I learned a lot from him. Highly rated by Hearst, he told me he was paid $10,000 in gold annually, no matter where he was in the world. When the 1939–45 broke out, Knickerbocker was one of the American correspondents who stuck it out in London and at a crucial time reported favourably on the situation in Britain. He stayed in the Savoy Hotel, entertained lavishly and persuaded his readers that, contrary to some opinion, we were in with a chance. Like Stuart Emeny, he had his career cut short by a fatal air crash.

The Americans fielded their A-team for this Abyssinian war. Jim Mills of Associated Press had already made his mark with the Rickett scoop. William Stoneman of the *Chicago Daily News*, who later took charge of the newspaper's London bureau, was also in the front rank, as was Ed Beatty of United Press. UP was not at the time seen as the most reliable of agencies, but because of Beatty I advised my foreign editor, Alastair Shannon, to take the service. The only portrait that exists of these American correspondents is the comic one in *Scoop*. They were better than that.

Four

When at last it came on 3 October, the outbreak of war took us all by surprise. We had risen early and gone to the palace to report the general mobilization ceremony. As this drew to a close, it was announced that Adowa had been bombed by Italian planes early that morning. There followed a bizarre scene. My version for readers of the *Morning Post* began:

> In brilliant sunshine, against a backdrop of green hills, chiefs, ready for war, had assembled in the palace yard. The Grand Chamberlain ascending the steps and standing between fluttering Ethiopian flags before the great Menelik war-drum began to read the proclamation.
>
> Even while he was reading, with a motionless sea of black faces below him, the news from Adowa was heard in whispers from all sides.
>
> An official, rising above the seething mass, struggled to obtain silence. At the top of his voice he tried to make the dread telegraph audible amid the clamour, and here and there a phrase penetrated the mad enthusiasm of the warriors. It was

stated that the Italians had bombed Adowa, and that women and children had suffered in the fighting.

The official reading the decree in French was Dr Lorenzo Taezaz, chief of the press bureau. He had difficulty in making himself heard above the din created mainly by the journalists. Waugh's version, which he will have enjoyed writing, carried a sharp rebuke for the reporters:

> He stood on a chair, a diminutive, neat, black figure, crying for attention. A great deal of noise came from the journalists themselves. I had seldom seen them to worse advantage. Dr Lorenzo had in his hand a sheaf of copies of the decree. The journalists did not want to hear him read it. They wanted to secure their copies and race with them for the wireless bureau. Lorenzo kept crying in French, 'Gentlemen, gentlemen, I have something of great importance to communicate to you.'
>
> He held the papers above his head and the journalists jumped for them, trying to snatch them like badly brought up children at a Christmas party.

That is a bit of Waugh humbug. He had no sympathy for the Abyssinian officials who dealt with the press and thought they were 'boobies' – a favourite word of contempt. But he had even less sympathy for his newspaper colleagues. Of course we wanted copies of the statement and quickly; it would be a busy day at the radio station. An official who thought we wished to hear him reading it to us first had no understanding of the press.

The bombardment of Addis Ababa, I went on to report, was expected at any moment. Instinctively, I went straight from the proclamation up to the British legation to get their reaction. I cannot remember what they had to tell me, but I may well have found it disappointing. According to a letter I wrote home (which I subsequently forgot about), I was the first person to inform Sir Sidney Barton, our minister, that war had broken out. When I saw him later that morning, he had heard nothing from his government. That sounds odd today when we are infested with communications, but the world of 1935 was far removed from the world of today, when Sir Sidney Barton would have known before any reporter that war had broken out. Furthermore, he would have sent his report on conditions in Addis Ababa to assist the Foreign Office to prepare a statement to be made in the House of Commons by the foreign secretary that same afternoon.

It emerged that the Italian attack had begun at sunrise as aircraft circled over Adigrat, fifty miles north-east of Adowa. The bombs that fell there wrecked a hundred houses. Damage to Adowa, scene of the battle of 1896 in which the Italians were heavily defeated, was less severe, and only fifteen houses were destroyed.

At first the Italians denied all this, declaring that the flights were for reconnaissance only. Count Ciano, Mussolini's son-in-law, had led one of the squadrons. Later, Italy admitted

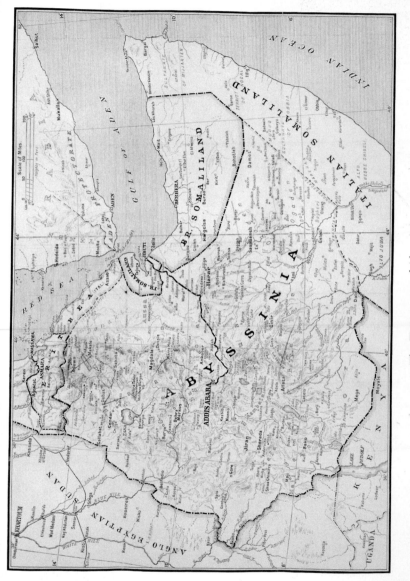

The *Times* map of Abyssinia.

THE MORNING POST.
15, TUDOR STREET,
LONDON, E.C.4.

TELEPHONE 1000 CENTRAL

TO ALL WHOM IT MAY CONCERN.

The Bearer of this is Mr. William
Francis Deedes, a member of the Staff of the
MORNING POST. He has been appointed
Special Correspondent for this paper in
Abyssinia, The Sudan, Somaliland and British
East Africa.

I shall be obliged for all permissible
facilities which may be granted him.

H. A. Gwynne
EDITOR.

AUGUST, 1935.

Letter of credentials from H. A. Gwynne, editor of the *Morning Post*. It bears the newspaper's seal on blue sealing wax.

My Sikh driver and his handsome Chrysler car outside the Deutsches Haus in Addis Ababa. The car was a gas-guzzler.

```
1   MILK  JUG

1   SOUP  STRAINER

MACARONI

1  BIG  FRYING  PAN

VINIGAR

1  BIG  KNIFE  FOR  COOKING

1  LITTLE  KNIFE  FOR  COOKING

1  BAKING  TIN

FLOUR

2 - 3 LARGE  COOKING  SPOONS
```

The shopping list which Waugh and I put together before our abortive trip to the north.

My press pass in Addis Ababa.

LION VAINQEUR DE LA TRIBU DE JUDA
HAILE SELLASSIE IER
ELU DU SEIGNEUR EMPEREUR D'ETHIOPIE

PROCLAMATION.

Le conflit qui existe entre l'Italie et Notre Pays depuis près d'une année a pris naissance à Walwal le 5 décembre dernier.

Nos soldats servant d'escorte à une commission internationale y ont été attaqués par la troupe italienne sur notre territoire.

L'Italie, ensuite de cette attaque, a exigé de nous des réparations et des excuses que nous avons refusées.

Et lorsque, après beaucoup de résistance de la part de l'Italie, nous avons pu, grâce à notre persévérance et aux efforts du conseil de la société des nations, porter ce différend devant les arbitres, ceux-ci à l'unanimité, ont reconnu que nous n'avions pas commis la faute que l'Italie nous imputait.

En conséquence, les arbitres ont refusé de nous condamner aux réparations et aux excuses que l'Italie nous demandait sans droit.

Mais l'Italie qui, depuis longtemps, ne cache plus sa volonté d'asservir Notre pays, s'apprête à l'attaquer.

Reniant la signature qu'elle a donnée au Pacte de la Société des Nations, violant la promesse de paix qu'elle nous a solennellement faite par le traité italo-éthiopien de 1928, réduisant à néant tous ses engagements internationaux et notamment le pacte de renonciation à la guerre.

L'Italie s'apprête à violer une seconde fois notre territoire. L'heure est grave !

Que chacun de vous se lève, prenne ses armes et accoure à l'appel du Pays pour le défendre !

Soldats !

Groupez-vous autour de vos chefs !

Obéissez leur d'un seul coeur et repoussez l'envahisseur !

Que ceux qui ne peuvent à cause de leur faiblesse ou de leurs infirmités, prendre une part active à cette lutte sacrée, nous assistent de leurs prières.

L'opinion du monde entier se révolte en présence de l'agression dirigée contre nous.

Dieu sera avec nous.

Tous debout! pour l'Empereur! pour la patrie !

Addis-Abeba, le 3 Octobre 1935.

RADIOTELEGRAMME

M Deedes care british consulate

Harrar

Indication de réception
Reçu à 1840
le 30/11/3

Indication de transmission

Nature du Radio	Origine	Numéro	Nombre de mots	Date	Heure de dépôt	Mentions de service
	London	325	9	29	1325	=

What about coming home =
Posterity ./.

(LEFT) Proclamation distributed in Addis Ababa on the day Italy invaded Abyssinia.

(ABOVE) Welcome telegraph from the *Morning Post* in London, suggesting return.

Leaving the house I shared with my uncle, Sir Wyndham Deedes, in Victoria Park Square, Bethnal Green, at the start of a fortnight's journey to Addis Ababa, my bedding roll beside me. The balance of my quarter of a ton of luggage is out of sight.

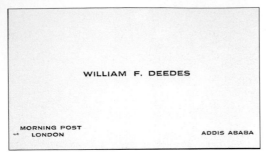

WILLIAM F. DEEDES

MORNING POST
LONDON   ADDIS ABABA

My visiting card,
printed in Addis Ababa.

Evelyn Waugh in
Palestine at Christmas,
1935. He had left Addis
Ababa, as he put it, 'To
hear the bells of Bethle-
hem on Christmas Day.'

The author, circa 1935.

Burial of the remains of Emperor Haile Selassie in November 2000, which took place in Addis Ababa seventy years after his coronation in 1930.

Photograph taken at the burial of Princess Tenangne Work,
the Emperor's only surviving child.

Outside the railway station in Addis Ababa in 2000.
It had remained virtually unchanged since 1935.

bombs had been dropped on Adowa, but denied the Abyssinian allegation that a hospital had been hit. Casualties were at first reported to be heavy. There was talk of 1,700 being killed or wounded. It turned out that Adowa had been practically empty when the bombers attacked. In this respect war has not changed at all; it is fought with statements and counter statements.

In Addis Ababa, we foresaw the prospect of an uneasy night. I thought it unlikely that Mussolini would bomb the capital, where his minister, count Vinci, was still in residence. My friend Stuart Emeny disagreed; he thought bombing was likely. After we had filed our copy he and I motored to the top of one of the hills surrounding Addis Ababa. After the sun went down, it was chilly and inhospitable. Some of our colleagues who shared Emeny's anxieties loaded trucks and made for the hills, where they planned to camp, but the government for reasons of its own had decided that no unauthorized person should leave the capital after nightfall. So the soldiers and police picketing all exits from the town sent them back.

Had I known then how destructive and terrifying bombing from the air can be, I would have been more troubled than I was. But, my imagination having nothing to feed on, I felt curiously detached from the prospect of air raids, and thought gratefully that if the Italians did attack the Abyssinian capital that night there would be ample time to write and file the copy next morning.

At this point I found the company of Evelyn Waugh a good deal more comforting than that of Stuart Emeny. Waugh had more experience than most of us of travelling in rough and risky parts of Africa. He liked to live comfortably – there was much of the sybarite about him – but as others grew nervous, he chose to treat the likelihood of Mussolini bombing us as a joke. There was more than one reason for this. Waugh's sympathies at the time lay more with Italy than with Abyssinia; he would have felt inclined to be reassuring about Italy's intentions. His disdain for his newspaper colleagues, which comes through so strongly in *Scoop*, was also a strong influence. The sight of them quivering at the prospect of being bombed afforded Waugh a good deal of satisfaction. There was a certain amount of: 'You may get better news stories than I do and stand in higher regard with your newspaper than I do with the *Daily Mail*, but when it comes to the point, you get the wind up and I don't!'

It delighted him to think that the American correspondents for all their bragging were timid at heart. I also think, it is fair to add, that his religious beliefs fortified him, and it was part of Waugh's character to treat as a joke what others found unacceptable. On top of all that, we know something about Waugh as a soldier in the Second World War. He was never popular with his brother officers nor was his army career distinguished, but no one associated with him on the dangerous mission he joined in Yugoslavia ever doubted his physical courage. His portrait of Major Hound in *Officers and Gentlemen* illustrates Waugh's contempt for timidity in battle. In his book *Eastern Approaches*, describing that bold adventure in Yugoslavia, Fitzroy Maclean writes: 'Randolph Churchill came over to see me before leaving for Croatia. With him came Evelyn Waugh, a new recruit, whose

Commando training and adventurous disposition made him a useful addition to the Mission.' Waugh had done his military training with the marines, and left them to join the commandos, something very few officers of his age would have dreamed of doing. On all these counts, which matter a lot in war, he was an excellent soldier, but he could not bring himself to submit to the discipline of senior officers of whom he did not approve. We get a glimpse of this in the opening of *Brideshead Revisited*. So, as a regimental officer he was difficult to handle; disenchantment set in. In Addis Ababa in 1935, the manners of the officers' mess did not count for much, but I found Waugh's martial qualities deeply reassuring.

After sending five cables and the best part of 500 words to the *Morning Post* through the cable office scrum, I felt pleasantly tired and slept dreamlessly under the Heft roof without a thought of air raids. At the age of twenty-two – as I also learned later from young officers with whom I served in the Second World War – sleep is a wonderful cushion against anxiety. Next morning the sun was shining and everything, even the apology for a garden which Mrs Heft kept, looked gorgeous.

As I have remarked, we had been unlucky at the sodden Masqal on 27 September, the day on which, proverbially, the rains in Abyssinia cease. But in the week between then and the outbreak of war a miracle had taken place. The rains had stopped, the sky had cleared and the flowers were bursting forth. Brilliantly coloured birds – East Africa is a region rich in bird life – suddenly appeared as though they had been awaiting this moment. It did not occur to me then, but on subsequent visits to Abyssinia at the same time of year I have thought of that passage from the Song of Solomon: 'Rise up, my love, my fair one, and come away. For, lo, the winter is past, the rain is over and gone; the flowers appear on the earth; the time of the singing of birds is come, and the voice of the turtle is heard in the land.' These lines could have been inspired by early October in Abyssinia.

'Spring and summer come as one here,' I wrote to my mother. 'There is no footling about through March, April and May. Last Sunday it poured with rain, was cold, wet and beastly, and the country looked perfectly frightful. Today and since Thursday it has been gorgeous. Addis is the ugliest capital in the world set in the world's most beautiful surroundings.' Sometimes amid scenes of more recent conflict, I have thought on some perversely beautiful day that the earth was silently mocking man's inhumanity to man.

What was happening elsewhere in the world we had no idea, and this was probably just as well. A week after the war started, the assembly of the League of Nations resolved by fifty sovereign states to one to take collective measures against Italy. Mussolini responded by saying that Italy would meet them with discipline, frugality and with sacrifice. He also made it plain that he would not tolerate sanctions which hampered his invasion of Abyssinia. He would respond to military sanctions 'with measures in kind'. Thus the world was given notice that effective sanctions against Italy would lead to war – and thereupon decided not to stand in Mussolini's way. Though few saw that far ahead, it was the beginning of the long slide towards the Second World War.

The mood of the British Labour party and trade unionists, by contrast, was ostensibly robust; hatred of fascism and the bloodshed in Abyssinia partly accounted for this. On 8 October, George Lansbury, a resolute pacifist, resigned his leadership of the Labour parliamentary group, giving way to Major Clement Attlee, who in the First World War had fought at the Dardanelles.

The Conservatives were gathered for their annual conference at Bournemouth on the day Mussolini bombed Adowa. A resolution was carried unanimously calling for rapid repairs to national defences and the reorganization of industry for speedy conversion to defence purposes, if need be. Stanley Baldwin, Conservative leader and second-in-command of the government to Labour's prime minister, Ramsay MacDonald, maintained that it was pointless for Britain to accept obligations under the covenant of the League of Nations unless the country had at its command adequate forces to carry them out.

At the far end of a telegraph line which seemed to deliver its messages as slowly as if they were in Morse code and where English mail took at least a fortnight to arrive, these international currents passed us by. October 4 fell on a Sunday. Crowds on the street cheered the Emperor as he drove from the palace to church. I cabled about 300 words, which under an arrangement made in the *Morning Post* office was transmuted into a thousand words of English prose. This is the right moment to introduce my most valued colleague in the *Morning Post* office, J. C. Trewin.

He had joined the newspaper as a reporter a year or two

after me, a slight, shy figure with some hesitation in speech and a beautiful prose style. The theatre was his main love, and he sometimes deputized for S. R. Littlewood, the *Morning Post*'s dramatic critic. We had friendly arguments about the merits of stage and screen. I persuaded him to come with me to see *The Petrified Forest* which was then showing at the Tivoli cinema in the Strand. He was polite about it, but not entranced.

Soon after war in Abyssinia broke out and the cost of my cables began to trouble the penurious *Morning Post*, they hit on a plan. I would send a summary of the day's events; Trewin would swot up Abyssinia, inhale the atmosphere and convert my summary into prose, rather as the classical writers described the Greek and Roman wars. The result was magical, and for me most flattering. For obvious reasons the newspaper could not let its readers into the secret, so Trewin's prose appeared every day under the byline of W. F. Deedes, the *Morning Post* special correspondent in Abyssinia. Bylines today are two a penny. In those days they rarely appeared over news stories and were counted a privilege. To have a byline over Trewin's prose was the tops.

When I learned of this arrangement, I sent a long letter of thanks to Trewin, which he must have kept, for not many years ago his son Ion, a notable figure in the world of book publishing, came across it and sent me a copy.

> 'Not only are your additions entirely without
> error,' I had written, 'but the stuff is just as I
> should like to have written it with time and space
> – but of course couldn't have done in a month of

*Sundays. Anyone would think you had lived your
life in Ethiopia. I feel ashamed to see the
miserable cables I transmit from here blossom
into such prose.*

*'I wish you were here to comment on the
flowers – God knows, there is nothing else to
write about . . . you'd be able to mail some
terrific articles. Coming back from Harar to
Diredawa the other day at 5 a.m., I saw the most
magnificent dawn you could possibly imagine.
What is more it broke over the east (as some
dawns do) and lit up what possibly will be a
battlefield. Even breakfastless and suffering from
innumerable bites after a sleepless night, it
seemed pretty good to me and I thought what fun
you could have had with it.*

*'There being no repertory theatre or theatre of
any kind here, you would be pretty miserable.
Shakespeare is unheard of; generally speaking,
the theatrical world of Ethiopia is at low ebb.'*

In Britain at that point a general election was taking place.
With a view to stirring up a bit of interest, I told Trewin, I had
tried to convince Abyssinian government officials that the
outcome would have the greatest effect on their cause. 'But
they only say they'd like to see what the Socialists could do,
and don't give a damn what happens anyway.' Abyssinia in
1935 was detached from the outside world in a way which
today is unimaginable.

I wrote nostalgically about my old drinking friends in Fleet Street – Trewin himself was an almost total abstainer – and asked after their health. 'Such daydreams one has. Here there are such restrictions. One can drink foul Italian Chianti with enough sediment to ditch a steam engine or St George beer, made locally and not bad, or brandy and crème de menthe mixed. Now that Evelyn Waugh and Patrick Balfour are away' – they were visiting Harar again – 'one has to drink even that by oneself.'

Happily, it was not my last partnership with Trewin; we worked together a year later on the *Morning Post* Christmas appeal for young children of the unemployed in the distressed areas. Trewin went off and moved our readers to tears about conditions among the unemployed in places like West Cumberland, Tyneside and South Wales, while I tried to raise the money.

Meanwhile the extraordinary position of the Italian minister in Addis Ababa, Count Vinci, presented the Abyssinians with a puzzle and offered journalists a welcome taste of honey. When the war long threatened by Italy became a virtual certainty from the last days of September onwards, Italy's minister might have been expected to pack his bags, close his handsome legation and return home. Vinci did nothing of the kind. He was a jolly fellow, but also a professional diplomat. In the days just before the war he was to be seen riding a horse in the capital alone or with a groom. He continued to do business and to entertain hospitably. His enemies declared he was trying to provoke an incident, but he had his own reasons for obstinately deciding to stay on. Italy had five consulates in different parts of Abyssinia – at Adowa, Gondar, Harar, Dessye and Debra Markos – each with two or three Europeans. In recent years, when travelling through the country, I have seen one or two of those former consulates. It must have been an extremely lonely life.

Early in September, Count Vinci had sought permission from the Abyssinian foreign office to withdraw his consuls. He received no satisfactory response. Eventually he was advised that all of them must return via Addis Ababa; they would not be allowed to travel more directly and conveniently towards the coast. This presumably was to stop them from observing troop movements. Permission for them to leave their posts was not finally granted until 22 September, so two consuls were still making their way slowly through the country when war broke out and Adowa was bombed.

In the circumstances Count Vinci felt he must stay on until all his men were safe, and he was still in Addis Ababa on 10 October, a week after war had started. Waugh's version was that after four years in an arduous post, Count Vinci felt he deserved a break and therefore decided to enjoy a few days of leisure before returning home and reporting for further duty. I think there was more to it than that. Vinci insisted that he was still awaiting the return of his commercial agent from Megalo, which he had every right to do, but the Emperor, not unreasonably, felt that he had had enough of the Italians and ordered his expulsion, unwisely adding charges of bad faith and abuse of diplomatic privilege. Vinci would leave, the authorities assured us, at 8 a.m. on 12 October. We rose at dawn and found a mounted guard of honour waiting outside the Italian legation. The Abyssinians desired the world to know that they did this sort of thing rather decently.

The diplomatic corps assembled at Addis Ababa railway station. Italian luggage appeared, including a caged leopard. But of the minister and his military attaché there was no sign. At the station, which was about eight miles from the legation, all was confusion. Signor Degrenet, the second secretary, escaped from a cordon of guards. He was chased and found with a revolver in his hand. Disarmed, he was returned to the station and put on the train. Eventually, without their minister, the Italian staff left three hours late, accompanied by a guard of forty Abyssinian soldiers. The diplomatic corps retired for a late breakfast. The Abyssinian foreign minister tried his luck at the Italian legation but to no avail. He went off to consult the Belgian minister, doyen of the diplomatic corps.

I reported twenty-four hours of intense activity in Addis Ababa to deal with a situation which had no diplomatic precedent. Vinci, who had locked himself in the cellar, had been removed from his legation at five o'clock the previous evening and kept under guard at the house of Ras Desta. A second train was produced in great secrecy. It was announced that Count Vinci would board it from the customs shed some two hundred yards from the station platform. At 10 o'clock all was in readiness, the train with steam up, but still no minister.

This second hitch had arisen not from Count Vinci's refusal to go, but because the Abyssinian government had changed its tactics. The Italian pair, Vinci and his military attaché

Calderini, remained in Addis Ababa for another fortnight. Their line was that while any of their staff remained in the country it was imperative for them to stay. Abyssinian mistrust had led to long delays in the safe return of the consuls. The Megalo agent had taken his time on a long march to a station on the railway line. There, eventually, Vinci's train picked him up.

Against the background of war this was small beer but for the journalists it was intoxicating; it was the best news story they had enjoyed since the Rickett affair and, happily, was more evenly distributed among them. I reported that the Abyssinian government had acted with tact and diplomacy. Waugh declared that the press bureau had done its best to humiliate Vinci, stating falsely that he had been unable to leave because he was in an alcoholic stupor. I doubt if any of us knew the full truth of the matter. To his credit, Vinci went off to Mogadishu where, according to Waugh's account, he commanded a company of native infantry with conspicuous success.

As things began to hot up, I was dismayed to receive a cable from the office requesting me to mail a profile of the Emperor. He was, after all, at the centre of the stage. Everyone was acquainted with Mussolini, who blew his own trumpet loudly, but knew next to nothing about Haile Selassie; he was not then the international figure he later became. My first impression was of a quaint, shy, possibly strong-willed figure of no great distinction who had suddenly and reluctantly become a figure in world politics.

Since his grand coronation in 1930, which the Duke of Gloucester and many international notables had attended, he had sunk back into obscurity. Paul Henze, who served in the United States foreign service was later to remark, 'Patience, a sense of mission, energy, statesmanship and a favourable concatenation of circumstances had brought Ras Tafari Makonnen to the Solomonic throne. He attributed his good fortune to God's will, but throughout his life he relied on the conviction that God helps those who help themselves.' Later on I came to realize that assessment was close to the mark, but in September 1935 I had formed no clear impression of his character. Waugh's portrait in *Black Mischief*, written after the coronation, of a young ruler anxious to modernize his anarchic state struck me as a possible view. But Waugh insisted, as he usually did, that his portrait of Seth, Emperor of Azania, was not drawn from any real person such as Haile Selassie. In fact his portrait of a busy modernizer was a fair one. A leading British expert on Abyssinia, Edward Ullendorf, later wrote of the Emperor, 'For two thirds of his life all the problems Haile Selassie had to face rose from the fact that he was in advance of his time.'

Everyone I consulted in Addis Ababa acknowledged the Emperor's dignified handling of this crisis for his country and admired his control of the wilder elements among his followers. He relied less than most rulers on his few advisers. A diplomat in Addis Ababa at the time remarked to me, 'As a politician in any cabinet in Western Europe, the Emperor would have won a name for himself, and would have made his influence felt by his quick brain and ability to get things done.'

I quoted an American businessman who told me, 'I can conduct more business with him in two hours than I accomplish in fifteen hours on Wall Street, where exist all the telephones, telegraphs and paraphernalia in the world for the transaction of rapid business.' What some of us mistook for shyness was in fact weariness. Because he was required to be a monarch, a diplomat and a businessman, Haile Selassie was compelled to take too much on himself, and what went on in Geneva in the days before war broke out would have tried the patience of a saint.

Worst of all, he knew he could not rely on the loyalty of his own kin. On 11 October, Dejazmatch Haile Selassie Gugsa, the Emperor's son-in-law and the ruler of eastern Tigray, defected with more than a thousand men; he had been in Italian pay for some time. In Addis Ababa, the news was at first received with incredulity. After a bit of burrowing, we found that Gugsa was a man with an axe to grind. He was jealous of his powerful neighbour, Ras Kassa, and nursed a long-standing grievance against the Emperor for having divided his territory on the death of his father and presented one portion of it to Ras Seyoum. Haile Selassie was a relatively enlightened emperor in a creaking feudal system struggling to prevail against a European power.

Five

For those journalists anxious about that critical balance between what they were costing and what they were proving to be worth to their newspapers, the outbreak of war brought no relief at all. My conscientious friend, Stuart Emeny of the *News Chronicle*, pointed out to Waugh and myself that we were nowhere near the fighting and so must appear to our newspapers even less useful than we had been before war broke out.

Emeny planted in my mind the possibility of our taking independent, if reckless, action. The attitude of the Abyssinian press bureau offered no early prospect of getting nearer to the war despite the fact that everyone knew that Italy had invaded Abyssinia and there was fighting in the north, probably in the south as well. Our newspapers knew this and expected us to be on the spot. Instead we were confined to Addis Ababa and fed with tendentious bulletins. Waugh was not unduly troubled by our predicament, but it bothered me. 'Outbreak of war here has robbed reporting of a good deal of initiative and made us more dependent on official statements,' I wrote to my foreign editor on 7 October. Our local 'spies' had become useless because the rumours they brought us no longer produced copy wanted in our newspaper offices. Our foreign desks were getting war news from Mussolini's front and looked to us to balance it with reliable reports from our end.

In mid-October the Abyssinian government did offer to allow correspondents to fly to the front, stipulating that they went at their own risk and in their own machines. I felt the offer would have limited appeal to the *Morning Post* because of the cost, but put the proposition to London. It would not have been difficult to arrange; Waugh, Balfour, Emeny and I would have shared the cost of one plane. There were planes and pilots standing by in Cairo and Khartoum for that sort of work. We could have flown north for a couple of days, looked around at whatever there was to see and come back to Addis to file our stories. My office was not encouraging. Having heard tales from Abyssinian pilots of what a flight to the north entailed, it was perhaps as well. H. R. Knickerbocker chanced his arm, persuaded some mercenary to fly him north, and wrote a lot about it. We admired his nerve, but seriously doubted whether he had seen very much.

Both sides insisted that their war was going according to plan. Mussolini's General de Bono was commanding an army of 100,000. Their advance in three columns appeared to be making good progress. Adigrat fell on 5 October, Adowa on 6 October. On our side, the Abyssinians declared themselves to be not in the least disheartened by this advance. Their initial retreat, I reported, was part of a preconceived plan. A government minister assured me that Italian troops would soon be fighting a rearguard action.

A week after the war had started, I wrote of an Abyssinian counter-attack. The bulk of the fighting had fallen to Ras Seyoum, a bold and ambitious leader who acted on his own initiative rather than orders from on high. The Emperor, I reported, had commenced the war with a purely defensive strategy but was yielding to those who favoured aggression and were urging him to move into Eritrea. At this point the Abyssinians decided to impose a form of censorship on us. They could hardly be blamed; some pretty wild stuff was going out. The reporter of one usually reliable news agency had reported 2,000 dead in Adowa. A blacklist of lying journalists had been drawn up and circulated to all government offices and legations. We were warned that henceforth our cables would be scrutinized and therefore, I predicted gloomily, subject to further delay.

The exodus from Addis began in earnest. At sunrise one morning I went down to the railway station and witnessed pitiable scenes. Greeks, Armenians, Egyptians and Italians accompanied by their numerous children were hastening towards the station, laden with baggage and precious possessions. 'The pity of it was,' I wrote, 'that three quarters of these people had no hope of getting seats on the train. All the accommodation in the Djibouti train – which holds only a hundred passengers – had been booked yesterday.

'Inside on the crowded platform 100 fortunate travellers, many of them still anxious for the safety of their seats, waited in a scene of astonishing confusion.

'Outside the heavy gates, the 300 or more people who had failed to secure admittance stood in a pathetic crowd by unwieldy bundles, brown paper parcels, battered tin trunks and heaps of miscellaneous baggage.'

It was my first experience of something I have since witnessed in many parts of the world – desperate people, with bewildered and frightened children, fleeing from conflict. It is the most wretched sight imaginable and always wrenches my guts.

Until the train left, those outside the heavy gates clamoured incessantly to enter the station. 'For more than three hours [I suspect these are the words of my friend Trewin] there was pandemonium – a polyglot babel of tongues, both inside and outside the station, the ceaseless crying of children, the barking of dogs, the shouting of station officials . . .' Eventually a troop of soldiers had to be called to disperse the crowd. The most painful sight was a carriage crowded with American children from the American Mission of Addis Ababa who were leaving for Egypt with their mothers. While their parents wept, the children laughed, waved at a man taking their photographs and playfully snatched off the hats of Abyssinian soldiers patrolling the platform. 'The streets of Addis Ababa were crowded far into the morning,' I reported, 'and some time elapsed before the thwarted travellers dispersed to their homes and lodgings – to wait for the coming of the next train a few days hence.'

By the third week in October some of us felt urgently in need of a change of air. Moreover, our offices were showing signs of disgruntlement. I received a cable: 'Interest fading. Curtail cabling somewhat unless possibilities good exclusives.' Patrick Balfour had extracted permission from the *Evening*

Standard to do a round trip via Djibouti, Zeila, Jijiga and then return home. His move made Evelyn Waugh restless; he suggested that we both went down to Harar, an ancient city of decaying beauty. Stuart Emeny, who had been sleeping outside the capital to avoid air raids heard of the plan and decided to join us. We cabled our newspapers, who wearily approved. We planned to leave on 23 October, a train day. I was convinced that Italy would soon open a southern front. If they did, we would be closer to the action in Harar than we ever seemed likely to get in the north.

We were looking forward to a comfortable expedition, but on the eve of our departure the British legation mentioned casually that every hotel in Harar had been closed, so we would have to stay in the British consulate compound camp there. That meant taking a lot more gear. Waugh and I spent the afternoon buying up plates and spoons and other camping supplies. I still have a copy of our shopping list, which runs: '1 milk jug, 1 soup strainer, macaroni, 1 big frying pan, vinegar, 1 big knife for cooking, 1 little knife for cooking, 1 baking tin, flour, 2–3 large cooking spoons . . .'

The four of us travelled together as far as Dire Dawa on a slow, stopping train. The first night was spent at Awash, a frightful spot where the only hotel seemed to have attracted every malarial mosquito and biting bug in the district. We dined with an agreeable Swedish officer who claimed to be in charge of the Awash bridge defences. Dire Dawa, our next stop, offered an improvement; the hotel ran to a bath for us all. Waugh was adept at procuring the comforts of life where they seemed least likely to be available. He discovered champagne in the hotel, rather bad champagne we all agreed, but the right stuff to revive our spirits. They made a tremendous fuss about producing it. I wondered when anyone in the hotel last had had the courage to ask for it.

Balfour went on to Djibouti that evening, but bequeathed me his servant. As Balfour was not returning to the country, my chances of holding on to this treasure seemed good. Gabri was useless at collecting information, but in terms of one's personal comfort he was matchless. One of his particular skills was buying quantities of cheap fruit. As we approached Dire Dawa he entered the compartment with fifteen bananas and a dozen tangerines which would have cost him a half-penny at the local station. He found spending money painful and grumbled unhappily in French at any purchases I made. '*Combien s'a coûte? C'est tres chère, monsieur!*' He spoke only French, but mine had improved enough for me to understand him. He made my bed, darned competently, looked after the luggage and undertook all the tipping and paying. For these services I paid him one pound a month.

After two days on the sluggish railway, we set off next morning for Harar and were saved hiring a motor truck by a Paramount film cameraman who was glad of our company. We piled into his vehicle – six Europeans, seven servants and a ton of luggage. The road, recently completed by a Swiss engineer, was terrible by European standards but the mountainous country was awesome and offered some startling vistas. For the first thirty miles we climbed steadily. As we rose the atmosphere became wonderfully clear. On such days it was possible to see a hundred miles and more across the Issa plain.

I could readily see the attraction Harar held for Waugh. As he has described it in *Waugh in Abyssinia*: 'For centuries before Menelik Harar was an independent Emirate, a city state founded by Arabs from across the Red Sea, who held sway over a large and fertile province inhabited by peaceable Moslem Gallas. They held the caravan route between the coast and the interior and made their city the emporium of a rich trade in coffee and slaves. The Harari people spoke their own language, wore distinctive costume, and exhibited a very high standard of culture in comparison with their rough neighbours . . . Even in 1935, after a generation of Abyssinian misrule and Indian and Levantine immigration, it retained something of the gracious fragrance of Fez or Meknes.'

This walled city had fallen a long way since its splendid days, so Waugh found it somewhat disappointing. Never having set eyes on anything comparable, I thought it enchanting. In contrast with what he called the 'straggling, nondescript, tin and tarmac squalor of Addis Ababa' it was refreshing, but what disillusioned Waugh, among many other things, was the growing proportion of Abyssinians to Hararis. It had become just another Abyssinian town. He had admired and hoped to see again the Harari girls, who had the slender grace of the Somalis. Instead, 'we found the bare, buttered, sponge-like heads, the dingy white robes, the stolid, sulky faces and silver crosses of the Abyssinian camp followers.' This was an inevitable consequence of the war; Abyssinian troops and their unavoidable companions had been pouring into Harar.

Fortunately, we had been wrongly advised about the hotel

situation. Waugh found a room at the Central, the only hotel within the walled city and pretty frightful but able to offer a bath; Emeny and I lodged at a pension just outside the town. There were other journalists in Harar, but they were thinner on the ground than in Addis Ababa. Unlike Addis, the city was on a war footing. No light could be shown after dark and the air-raid precautions were strict. Shamefully more interested in what Harar might produce by way of exclusives for my news-paper than in its ancient origins, I looked at the place through spectacles wholly different from Waugh's. The *Morning Post* headlined the long piece I wrote from there, 'Harar a City of Panic'. So indeed it was. More than half the population had fled, leaving only 10,000, of its 25,000 residents.

A stumbling walk I took after dark was a foretaste of what some English cities would be like in 1939–45. 'Travel after curfew within the walls of Harar,' I wrote, 'is as unpleasant as it is dangerous.' I was young and foolish enough to attempt to walk from the centre of town to the city gate around the hour of midnight. In the course of 500 yards, I was halted at the point of a rifle seventeen times. From doorways, hidden sentry boxes and the street shadows, I reported, 'Ethiopian figures leapt out at the sound of footsteps and the sight of a forbidden torchlight with the conventional cry: "Halt!"'

The nervous defenders of Harar assumed that anyone white was probably Italian, so, when challenged, the first thing to do was establish firmly one's nationality. One's footfall in the dark might also herald the approach of an officer inspecting the guard, and as a result one was greeted with a challenge of alarming vigour and ferocity. There was also the risk of disturbing sleeping sentries, whose first reaction on being awoken by footsteps might be to fire a round or two. The venture illustrated the extent to which failure to meet our newspapers' expectations had begun to drive some of us slightly mad. This, my second long piece from Harar, was headlined, 'Our Special Correspondent's Tour by Night'. Well, I reflected with satisfaction, when a copy of the newspaper eventually reached me, it *was* an exclusive.

I also made a tour of the medical facilities and found them hopelessly inadequate. There were only three small hospitals, none of them ready for field casualties. Almost every roof, however, bore a red cross; there were more red crosses than hospital beds. They were painted on houses, they told me, that had been requisitioned for possible use as hospitals. I wondered what the Italian pilots would make of them. 'Hitherto,' I reported on 28 October, 'no wounded have been brought to the town, but when fighting creeps north and casualties overwhelm Dr Hockman's modest camp near Jijiga, sick and wounded will arrive at Harar in numbers which the town will be utterly incapable of handling.'

The facilities were hopelessly understaffed. A doctor at the Swedish mission told me there were only two other doctors besides himself in the whole town, with about sixty European or Abyssinian volunteers with basic medical training. A single bombing raid would engage all the city's resources. To evacuate the wounded to Addis Ababa would involve a fifty-mile journey over rough roads to Dire Dawa and then a day or two on the railway. 'In the event of serious fighting in the south,' I reported, 'the hospital conditions will be too terrible to contemplate.' Alas, that proved to be one of my more accurate predictions.

We gave ourselves time, under Waugh's guidance, to look round this former city state. It still had many attractions, including silversmiths and other craftsmen and a few ancient beautiful houses. If you half-closed your eyes and ignored the decay, you could imagine the sort of city it once had been. Waugh decided he must stay on for a few more days, so Stuart Emeny and I made the return journey alone. To catch the Sunday train leaving Dire Dawa for Addis Ababa at 8 a.m. we had to rise at four in the morning. I grumbled a good deal at this, but our reward was seeing a majestic dawn rise behind the mountains.

We stopped at Afdem for lunch and there had a big surprise. As Emeny and I were crossing the railway line, another train drew in from the opposite direction. A head poked out from behind a blind and said, 'Goodbye!' It was Count Vinci, the Italian minister who, unknown to us, had left Addis Ababa the previous morning. He was travelling on a train stiff with armed guards and police who we were not allowed to approach, but we exchanged a few words with him through the window of his compartment. After the earlier excitement in Addis Ababa, it was a strange encounter. We were unlikely ever to see him again, I told Stuart Emeny.

The change had done us good and, as I reminded the ever-conscious and restless Emeny, if things started up in the south, we would be able to describe the town at the centre of it all. We returned to the capital and the mean diet of pronouncements from Dr Lorenzo's press bureau. The word around the capital was that the Emperor would shortly proceed north and make his headquarters at Dessye. When he went north, the press would be allowed to accompany him. This glad news was qualified by a warning that we must avoid mentioning the Emperor, troop movements, all war news outside the official communiqués, and anything that might assist the enemy or reflect adversely on Abyssinia's way of life. Anything infringing these conditions would simply be excised from our copy.

In the context of more recent experiences, none of these rules was wholly unreasonable. In any conflict today, the press might well be asked not to print material which might assist the enemy, nor to disparage the values which the country believed it was defending. But to the newspapermen assembled in Addis Ababa in late October 1935, being begged by their newspapers for war copy, they were a red rag to a bull. An emergency meeting of the Foreign Press Association was summoned at which we threatened to seek recall from our offices unless the terms were withdrawn and we were granted a new censor. We were engaged in a bloodless war of our own with Abyssinian officials who had no experience of dealing with such an enemy, but it was a war that brought no comfort at all to our news-hungry bosses.

However, there were still some weird war scenes to be reported from Addis Ababa. One bright morning the so-called Central Army paraded before their Emperor on a plain below the palace. Brandishing their weapons and shouting war cries, they marched past for hours, indulging in antics which would have given a British sergeant major a nervous breakdown. All work ceased in the capital as the population turned out to watch this spectacle. Alas, these hill men represented Abyssinian fighting forces of earlier days. With their lion-skin capes and brilliant accoutrements, they caught the eye but were, one suspected, wholly unequal to modern warfare. It struck me that about one man in ten looked over the age of sixty and one in five seemed over forty. Some were dressed as civilians. A few had straggling white beards. Most of them, I was told, nursed the illusion that, wherever fighting had taken place, the Emperor's men had won glorious and decisive victories. That seemed saddest of all.

At the end of October, Stuart Emeny and I picked up a story about Abyssinia's financial resources. We reckoned the country had at its disposal some £75 million to spend on the war. In today's money that would be about £3.5 billion or one sixth of the British peacetime defence budget. Most came from the Emperor's private fortune. Our facts were challenged but not disproved. The war chest, we reported, would buy rifles and ammunition from Belgium, heavier guns from Czechoslovakia. Very little of it, perhaps £10,000 privately subscribed, was destined for the Red Cross. The government, I reported, seemed heedless of the crime it was committing in neglecting the medical care of its troops. They would, as I witnessed a little later, pay a severe penalty for this error.

On the fifth anniversary of his accession to the throne, early in November 1935, the Emperor and Empress drove to St George's church where for four hours they took part in a form of Coptic mass and gave thanks. At such an hour, I found the chorus of praise and thanksgiving in which they were joined by a huge congregation strangely moving.

At about the same time one began to sense that the unreasonable hopes, or rather illusions, of the Abyssinian leaders were slipping away. Mussolini replaced de Bono with the more ruthless Pietro Badoglio. Makale, where heavy fighting had been expected, fell suddenly. Italian communiqués, which had proved pretty accurate, spoke of rapid advances. In Addis Ababa, they were countered by silence. It seemed imperative to find out what was happening, and this propelled Stuart Emeny, Evelyn Waugh and myself into our first – and last – great adventure.

Six

I remained convinced that if we were going to see any fighting, the south was the place to be. My instructions from the office, however, were to remain at 'headquarters', wherever that might be. So when we heard that the Emperor would be going north to Dessye and that we would be allowed to accompany him, I decided that was the place to go.

Emeny and Waugh were already working on the trip. They had hired a Chevrolet truck from a dubious Syrian character named Karam, whose financial position was so precarious he lacked the wherewithal to equip the lorry with spare parts or even petrol. Indeed, after we had hired it and filled it with petrol, he let it out to a building contractor to raise enough money for a spare tyre. Coming in late, I was spared these transactions. Waugh had done most of it. The cost involved seemed reasonable. All in, a fortnight at Dessye would amount to 600 thalers or about fifty pounds – say £2,000 today.

Waugh and his servant James set about recruiting suitable staff for the expedition. A good cook was important and in that department Waugh could be trusted to make the right choice. But we had trouble with the driver; given an advance on his wages, he got drunk on *tej* and bought a gun. Then, as I reported in a letter home, 'in a state of great pie-eyedness he loosed off his gun and is now reposing in gaol.' I thought my Sikh chauffeur might fill the vacancy, but the other servants vetoed him – he was a very superior individual. A substitute was eventually found on the eve of our departure. Together with the cook's boy that meant a retinue of six servants. Our Chevrolet was capable of carrying a ton, but with forty gallons of gasoline, enough food for a fortnight, tents and nine of us, to say nothing of the heavy going, it would be tested.

On learning of our intentions, various locals came to us begging for a seat in the truck. Most of them volunteered to become slaves and do whatever we wanted for nothing; none of them were the slightest use. Emeny and Waugh sat like magistrates in court examining these people. I had my doubts about the cook, but as they seemed happy with him, I kept silent. Herr Heft, proprietor of the Deutsches Haus, became restive. He saw a small fortune motoring away from him. All these years on, I look back on the Hefts as benefactors but that was not how we felt at the time. 'For two months,' I wrote, 'we have beaten and blasphemed him into comparative servility and now get goodish service and not-too-bad food. Occasionally he lapses and serves a filthy meal. Then we go out and buy tins and eat a meal on our own. That jars him and he rallies. So it goes. His wife has been dying of pneumonia for some while, which may make a difference. But today I heard a rumour she was never ill at all, but has run off to get away from him. That too might make a difference.'

On the eve of departure, the Italians suddenly launched an

attack in the south. The Reuters man and George Steer of *The Times* dashed off there. My young friend Dick Sheepshanks, whom I had recently watched scoring a fine innings for Eton against Harrow at Lord's, arrived to assist the Reuters representative. He promptly went down with dysentery picked up in Djibouti and seemed destined for home. We heard that injured and retreating Abyssinians were pouring back through Harar. But then, I reflected, they may well be pouring back through Dessye as well, so I elected to stay with the Chevrolet.

There was no road as such to Dessye, only a caravan track. Most people reckoned it would take us four days hard travelling to get a motor vehicle there, which meant three cold nights on the road. Dust, they warned us, would probably lead to engine trouble and breakdowns. We dismissed these cares lightly. Our press cards were endorsed, our servants were granted passes. All seemed set fair for our departure on the morning of 13 November, the day designated by the press bureau. Other press parties had been making preparations similar to our own. Waugh wrote about one of the largest vehicles splendidly emblazoned with the Lion of Judah and the legend '——Co. Inc. of New York EXPEDITION TO THE FRONT WITH H.M. THE EMPEROR OF ETHIOPIA'.

Yet there lurked in our minds doubts as to whether this expedition would ever be allowed to set forth. On the eve of departure, 12 November, there was no word of postponement and we resolutely decided to set forth early next morning with or without the rest of the caravan. Waugh has described in *Waugh in Abyssinia* what happened next morning with a wealth of detail I had forgotten:

Most of the loading was done on the day before. That night we kept the lorry in the road outside the Deutsches Haus and put two boys to sleep in it. We meant to start at dawn, but, just as we were ready, James accused the cook of peculation, the Abyssinians refused to be driven by a Harari, and my personal boy burst into tears. I think they had spent the evening saying goodbye to their friends and were suffering from hangovers. The only two who kept their composure were those who had guarded the lorry. It was nearly nine before everyone's honour was satisfied. The streets were then crowded and our lorry, painted with the names of our papers and flying the Union Jack, made a conspicuous object. We drove past the press bureau, glancing to see there was no notice on the door. We let down the side curtains, and the three whites lay low among the cases of stores hoping that we should pass as government transport.

It is vain as one grows older to try to explain the mood which at the age of twenty-two leads you into foolhardiness. I remember the excitement of motoring unchecked out of Addis Ababa, of knowing that we were putting one across the intolerable press bureau. I felt confidence in Waugh's ability to bluff us out of a tight corner. His ability to intimidate friend or foe was impressive; his curt manner with our servants got far better results than the diffidence Emeny and I showed towards them. Emeny was enterprising but nervous, as he had shown over the non-existent air raids, whereas Waugh's grand manner suggested that he would make any Abyssinian warrior who stood in our path look small. Without Waugh our modest adventure would probably not have taken place. Am I saying that he led us into mischief? No, but my impression is that without his leadership neither Emeny nor I would have had the self-confidence to attempt the expedition. Waugh was endowed with many of the qualities that good officers are supposed to possess. Why, I have often wondered since, was his later career in the army so disappointing?

Until we were clear of the city, we remained hidden. It seemed reasonable to expect that on reaching the city boundary we would encounter a military checkpoint. There was nothing of the kind. After an hour of great discomfort as the lorry struggled over uneven ground, the servants gave us the all-clear. We sat up and looked out over the country. There was no sort of road; we were picking our way along a rough track occasionally marked with stones. The local population, which was thin on the ground, showed no interest in us though they can seldom have set eyes on a motor vehicle.

At one point we came across what appeared to be a trailing telephone wire. We cut it with a pair of pliers. It has lurked at the back of my conscience ever since as our only nefarious act. We knew that sooner or later orders would go up the line from Addis Ababa to stop us. Cutting the wire seemed a good way of thwarting them. We drove on unimpeded until the early afternoon and were about fifty miles from Addis before the first provincial telephone post we had encountered stopped us.

We explained the situation and displayed papers and passes, all of them in order. They told us that a message had been sent from Addis Ababa to northern stations to hold up our vehicle, by force if necessary. We were to return at once. All this had slowly to be interpreted through Waugh's James. Itching to get moving again, I lost track of the negotiations. According to Waugh, the man in charge of the telephone at this post declared that he had been ordered to stop two lorry loads of white men travelling without permits. But we were accompanied by no other vehicle and we had permits. It turned out later that the Emperor had been apprised of our departure one hour after we had left Addis Ababa. He had ordered troops and cars to be mobilized and every post contacted to stop us.

Unaware of this, we surmised that the message to the telephone post might be a hoax, sent by a jealous colleague, so we asked them to tell us who had sent the message. Could we have it in writing? The telephone man refused to enlighten us. The matter was then referred to the local chief. After examining our papers, he said, 'I cannot possibly hold you; all your papers are in order.' Waugh reckoned that the chief distrusted messages down the telephone as much as we did. He could see that our passes were valid and that was good enough. To seal this amicable settlement, James poured several fingers of whisky into a mug which we gave to the chief. He downed it, blinked, apologized for the inconvenience we had been caused and waved us on our way.

The telephone man, overruled by his chief, was furious. He rang up Addis Ababa and put them in a frenzy by declaring that we had burst through the post by force and refused to stop. It was totally untrue, but it sounded bad and strengthened their determination to stop us at all costs. This was a capital offence. The encounter had cost us half an hour in the late afternoon. We decided we must make camp before darkness fell and after another hour on the road we turned off and stopped for the night. We had two tents, a big one belonging to Emeny which we two shared, and Waugh's smaller one. With the help of the six servants we had the tents up, beds arranged and the kitchen in working order by sunset. We had been warned about the cold, but it was fiercer than we had expected. A howling wind drove across the plain and penetrated everything. Food was cold two minutes after it had been cooked and our blankets might as well have been sheets.

But after preliminary difficulties with the Primus stoves, our cook excelled himself, producing omelettes and cooked meat and finishing with some excellent coffee. We had finished the meal by eight o'clock, and because the cold made sleep uninviting, Waugh and Emeny decided we would attempt to play three-handed bridge. At the best of times this is not a satisfactory game; when one of the trio has never played bridge, it affords no satisfaction at all. Seldom in my life have I been more miserable. I fumbled my cards with frozen fingers and Waugh and Emeny, both good players, became impatient. Waugh grew irascible. All thoughts of our precarious situation, of being hunted by furious officials from Addis Ababa, were banished by my panic over this barmy card game.

The servants made no attempt to sleep but sat chattering

round the embers of a fire. We rose at 4 a.m., an hour before dawn, ate a rough breakfast and struck camp. Our plan was to approach Debra Birhan by stealth very early in the hope that they might not be fully awake. It was the last telephone station on our road, and if we could clear it, the way on to Dessye would be open. By 5.30 a.m., with a glint of sun on the horizon, we got going. But the track we were on was hard going and we did not reach Debra Birhan, some eighty miles from Addis Ababa, until 9 a.m., by which time, roused by messages from Addis Ababa, they could hardly have been wider awake. Hoping to pass off the Chevrolet as a local vehicle, Waugh, Emeny and I again hid among the baggage and the boxes and pulled a tarpaulin over our heads. The drawback was that we could not see where we were going nor give the driver guidance. We could only hear the lorry being ordered to halt and then a fierce altercation between James and the locals.

Clearly we were not going to get through by stealth, so, feigning the appearance of men who had just woken from deep asleep, we emerged from our hiding place looking pretty silly, and introduced ourselves. The suddenness of our appearance and the general fishiness of the proceedings made one or two men raise their rifles; but they were calmed by their chief, whom I described in a letter home as 'a one-eyed bird of great ferocity and nastiness'.

In Abyssinian fashion, both sides at first adopted postures of mateyness. No mention was made of our dash from Addis Ababa; the chief said nothing about the telegrams he had been receiving about us. We were halted at the centre of a large village, with a church and the chief's residence nearby. A gaggle of unkempt soldiers surrounded us, all of them armed with unreliable-looking weapons. We accepted an invitation to enter the chief's small headquarters and displayed our papers and permits. This seemed to be well received. Ah, yes. We could proceed most assuredly, but it would not be right to send us on our way without a further note of permission and recommendation to his friends further along the road. At this point James observed quietly to Waugh, 'I think, sir, that this is a liar-man.'

It was a great game of bluff, in which we were destined to be on the losing side. But, soothed by the chief's solicitude, we relaxed and sat awaiting his note of permission. After an hour, we became slightly restive and enquired whether the note was yet sealed and ready. We sweetened our request with a stiff glass of whisky. Unfortunately, the chief was unable to partake because this was a fast day. I had prepared his drink, and if it had not been a fast day we might well have been on our way to Dessye. After declining our drink, the chief explained to us that purely as a matter of routine he had telephoned Addis Ababa to tell them that our vehicle was passing through the village. Not then aware of the uproar going on in Addis over our departure, we thought this sounded reasonable enough and settled down. After two more hours, we became restive again and made a fresh approach to the chief.

He at once became solicitous, and said that on account of our being such great men it was unfitting that we should be left standing about in the sun. Would we not erect our tent and make ourselves comfortable? It was the last thing we wanted to do; we wanted to get moving before the web being woven round us grew thicker. But it seemed wise to comply. It was conceded that our papers were entirely in order and we had the right to proceed to Dessye, but, it was pointed out, we had – doubtless inadvertently – failed to get the necessary permission to leave Addis Ababa. That was the hitch.

We set up the tent and ate lunch. Then Waugh and I decided to take a stroll through the village. We discovered huge barricades of stones and tree trunks at either end of the road. These, we were told, were to keep the savage men from harming us. It then became apparent to us that the chief was emphatically not on our side. That was not all. 'Armed chaps,' I reported home later, 'very decrepit indeed, but armed, were called out and formed a jolly little semi-circle round our tent.' All attempts to negotiate terms proved fruitless. We asked if we could send off a few messages, to Lorenzo at the press bureau, to Mr Colson, American adviser to the government and a friend, to the British legation. All these requests were refused. It became clear to us that we had been hoodwinked from the start. From the moment the old chief clapped eyes on us, he knew the game to play.

Yet an undercurrent of nervousness ran through him. Waugh's interpreter, James, had imparted this to us. 'He is a little afraid,' he said. 'You must pretend to be very angry.' We rejected this advice and on perceiving we had no option but to spend the night at Debra Birhan we set up the other tent. This docility alarmed the chief. He was not to know that we were unarmed. He judged we might well try to shoot our way out after dark, so he sought to separate us from our vehicle. We were, he declared, on a cold and dangerous camping ground; we might be attacked. Would we not like to move to a more sheltered spot? No, we said, we wished to remain where we were.

In his account of the affair, Waugh declares they then tried a stupendous lie. The Emperor had been on the telephone, they announced, saying that ten lorry loads of journalists were on their way to join us. If we waited until morning, we could all travel on together. We shrugged and settled down for the night, surrounded by men from the village fiddling with the bolts of their rifles. The chief set up his own tent nearby to keep an eye on us. It was bitterly cold again but we had the meagre satisfaction of knowing they were less snugly camped than we were.

Next morning, the chief appeared to tell us in no uncertain manner that we were to return to Addis. He was armed with a telegram sent by an official at the palace which accused us of all manner of offences. The barrier on the road behind us was lifted. I harboured the fear that on our way back we would pass a caravan of virtuous journalists who had played by the book. Mercifully, we met nobody. By forcing the pace a bit, and unimpeded by negotiations at frontier posts, we made Addis Ababa before dark, returning gratefully to our warm beds at Mr and Mrs Heft's lodging house.

Our minister, the good Sir Sidney Barton, was inclined to be shirty about our adventure. Most of the legation staff were delighted and expressed the hope that it would liven up the Abyssinian government. Officials partly responsible for the muddle began with dark looks, but made it up with a hand-shake. The Emperor was said to have come round to thinking it rather a good show and had laughed a bit. A generous race, the Abyssinians.

My account in the *Morning Post* appeared under the main headline, 'Up the Line with the Abyssinians', with a sub-heading, 'Our correspondent held prisoner'. 'After three adventurous and somewhat hazardous days in the interior,' I wrote, 'I succeeded in penetrating 100 miles north in the only caravan which has so far left Addis Ababa.'

After explaining the circumstances of our arrest, using a rather broad brush I went on, 'I was able to investigate rumours of the reasons for the postponement of the visit to Dessye, and I obtained a first-hand view of Ethiopian troops bound for the north. At Debra Birhan I learned that the fighting which broke out among the uniformed and non-uniformed soldiers en route for Dessye practically consisted of mutiny and led to bloodshed among the troops. The trouble was caused by the jealousy of the shamma-clad Ethiopians of the uniformed and armed soldiers . . .' Well, I said to myself as I sent it off, it *is* more or less exclusive.

Forgiveness for our escapade must have been swift, for within forty-eight hours of our return Waugh and Emeny were on the same road again, this time with full permission and accompanied by a number of other colleagues. I felt I had seen enough of the north, and decided to pay the southern front one more visit. George Steer of *The Times* and the Reuters man took the same decision. We travelled with two attractive ladies from Spanish newspapers; it was as well they accompanied us for, as I had foreseen, Harar's hospital arrangements proved totally inadequate. The Italians had been dropping mustard gas in the south, which produced serious blistering and blood poisoning in the Abyssinians who encountered it. Shocked by what they saw in Harar's so-called hospitals, both women put their newspapers on hold and turned themselves into auxiliary nurses.

In terms of sniffing out the action, I did a degree better than Waugh and Emeny. Towards the end of November, Waugh wrote unhappily to his parents from Dessye complaining, 'We get absolutely no news from outside. The war may be over for all we know.' He thought, astonishingly, that the Italians were beaten. At least on the southern front I knew better than that.

Waugh wrote even more unhappily to his friend Penelope Betjeman, the subject of one of his more tortured relationships. She had been alarmed, according to Martin Stannard's account, when, both before and after her marriage, Waugh made advances to her. 'I remember being very shocked as he was a practising Roman Catholic . . . He never attracted me in the very least.' 'I am in a bitterly cold mountain,' Waugh wrote to her 'with a boring hypochondriac socialist. God I could kill him.' This was poor Stuart Emeny and shows the dark side of Waugh's nature. He got on well enough with Emeny, but in speaking or writing about him, as I have mentioned before, he referred to him contemptuously as 'the Radical' or 'a socialist'. The cold wind on the Dessye road must have affected his liver, for his letter to Penelope Betjeman continues: 'The telegraph very sensibly refuses to accept press cables any more. I am a very bad journalist, well only a shit could be good at this particular job.'

Waugh had told me earlier of his intention to hear the bells of Bethlehem at Christmas, and although I cannot be sure because we parted in Abyssinia, he presumably achieved this, for he sent a postcard to Katharine Asquith on 23 December from Jerusalem. At the end of November, the *Morning Post* cabled me in Harar and suggested I return to England for Christmas. About half of the hundred correspondents who had come to Abyssinia to report the war were already back.

As I travelled to London and Waugh to Jerusalem, word reached us of the Hoare-Laval pact. This in effect would buy off Italy with about a third of its victim's territory. At first, amazingly, the British cabinet backed the plan, but it led to a political storm and the resignation of the Foreign Secretary, Sir Samuel Hoare.

Back in London I recovered my taste for journalism by reporting the lying-in-state of King George V, who had died at Sandringham in January 1936, and an unauthorized strike at Smithfield market involving 9,000 men, which created a serious meat shortage for several days. I found it reassuring after five months away from the office to be entrusted with such stories and to see once again above what I wrote 'By our Special Representative'. At least, I reflected, it is all my own work, and not ghosted from skeleton cables by the talented J. C. Trewin.

Gradually, the Italian forces advanced and the Abyssinians disintegrated. Once or twice, the *Morning Post* called upon its 'Special Correspondent lately in Abyssinia' to comment on the course of the war. In April, Abyssinia made a final desperate call to arms. On 2 May 1936, the Emperor boarded a train for Djibouti with his small entourage of nobles and officers. Forty-eight hours later they were on the British warship *Enterprise*, bound for England. The Lion of Judah went into exile. On 5 May, Badoglio's forces, preceded by a violent thunderstorm, made their triumphal entry into Addis Ababa. By then we had almost forgotten Abyssinia. Hitler had invaded Rhineland and the Spanish Civil War was upon us. I was directed to examine the state of British defences.

But on his arrival at 6 Prince's Gate in London, I had a final sight of the Emperor. He sat silent while an official read to the assembled press his testimony. 'We have never desired war. It was imposed upon us. Devastated fields and villages . . . the bodies of the aged and of the women and children . . . rule of force over right.' Exceptionally, the subeditors allowed me to open my news story poetically with lines from *Paradise Lost*:

> With grave
> Aspect he rose, and in his rising seem'd
> A pillar of state; deep on his front engraven
> Deliberation sat and public care;
> And princely counsel in his face yet shone,
> Majestic though in ruin.

Seven

Having spent part of my life brushing aside the charge that I was the model for William Boot, and recalling some of the attributes with which Evelyn Waugh endowed his characters in *Scoop*, I have formed ideas of my own on how he composed his portraits. In common with almost all great novelists he rarely drew characters directly from real life, but dressed them up with the attributes and idiosyncrasies of people he knew or had met, whom he liked or disliked.

As for William Boot, I have always conceded that being generously saddled by the *Morning Post* with quarter of a ton of baggage, which Waugh – living out of a suitcase – thought risible, I may have contributed something to his jokes about cleft sticks and canoes. But many of us, particularly the Americans, went overburdened with kit. This, as I pointed out earlier, was because so little was known in our native lands about conditions in Abyssinia. Waugh, having reported the Emperor's coronation in 1930, was better informed. He knew that tropical kit and snake-bite lotion would be extraneous in Addis Ababa, 8,500 feet above sea level. It is also conceivable, I have sometimes added diffidently to inter-rogators, that my inexperience and naivety as a reporter in

Africa might have contributed a few bricks to the building of Boot.

There the resemblances end. Boot Magna Hall was far removed from my world. I was incapable of writing a nature note. I have always surmised too that the German girl Katchen, who made such a fool of William, could well have been a whisper in Waugh's ear from his publishers Chapman & Hall, who felt even in those days that a novel needed a whiff of sex interest. What I know for certain is that nothing in the least like Katchen came my way in Addis Ababa. She has always seemed to me the shallowest of Waugh's characters in *Scoop*, perhaps because she seems to have been pure invention and not drawn from anyone we encountered. The improbable figure of Mr Baldwin was not pure invention; he was what Francis Rickett with his grandiose plans for acquiring Abyssinia's mineral rights might so well have been to Waugh, had things turned out a little differently.

On the other hand, the brush strokes portraying the central figure of Lord Copper, who unwittingly became William Boot's employer, repay study. There were half a dozen press lords in the mid-1930s from whom Waugh might have drawn inspiration, but I think we can eliminate Lord Riddell of the *News of the World*, Lord Camrose of *The Daily Telegraph* and his brother, Lord Kemsley, who owned the *Sunday Times Sunday Graphic* and *Daily Sketch*. They were simply too competent to qualify. That leaves us with the first Lord Rothermere, proprietor of the *Daily Mail* and so Waugh's employer in Abyssinia, and Lord Beaverbrook, proprietor of the *Daily* (and *Sunday*) *Express*, where Waugh had worked briefly as a probationer in 1927 before getting the sack. (He had not proved one of their 'discoveries'. Only one piece he wrote appeared in the paper – and that was alleged to have been stolen from another newspaper – and after five weeks he was out.) But Beaverbrook's garish office of black glass in Fleet Street, which Waugh would have known, could well have inspired Lord Copper's grand Megalopolitan building at 700–853 Fleet Street.

The *Daily Mail* and the *Daily Express*, rivals and both then broadsheets, were obviously the models for *The Brute* and *The Beast*. Furthermore, both Rothermere and Beaverbrook exhibited in their different ways the *folie de grandeur* of Copper, each seeking to lord it over politicians. Beaverbrook, like Copper, considered himself matchless – justifiably so – at spotting journalists of great potential, and certainly kept his staff on their toes. Beverley Baxter, Arthur Christiansen, John Gordon, John Junor, Sefton Delmer, Rene MacCall were all Beaverbrook men. But he was altogether smarter than Copper. To complete the portrait, I think we must add the ghost of Rothermere's elder brother, Lord Northcliffe. Before he died tragically, mentally deranged and attended by nurses under the direction of Lord Horder, Northcliffe was already exhibiting some of Copper's eccentricities – his megalomania, his habit of giving peremptory and ridiculous orders to underlings.

Mr Salter, Lord Copper's luckless foreign editor at the *Daily Beast*, is harder to place, but only because there were so many like him in the Fleet Street of the mid-1930s. People showed more deference to their employers in those days, particularly if their employers were whimsical press lords. We had a reporter on *The Daily Telegraph* who invariably worked the last watch between 5 p.m. and 1 a.m. Throughout this stint he kept a trilby hat on his head, unless Lord Camrose called the reporters' room on the telephone in which case he automatically whipped it off to take the call.

The busy Mrs Stitch, who provided the foundation for Waugh's comedy by persuading Copper to employ the wrong Boot, is said to be a likeness of Lady Diana Cooper, actress, beauty and wife of Alfred Duff Cooper, who was a cabinet minister and a friend of Waugh's. But, like Lord Copper, Josephine Stitch and her ways embody more than one character. When driving her small car down the steps of the gentlemen's lavatory in Sloane Square, she seems far removed from the statuesque Diana Cooper I saw playing the lead in *The Miracle*, the spectacular religious play which ran successfully at the Lyceum Theatre in London in 1932 and which went on tour the following year. In *Scoop* she seems rather to have been plucked from the pages of Waugh's earlier satire *Vile Bodies*.

It is when we come to Waugh's caricatures in *Scoop* of the journalists whom he encountered or worked with in Abyssinia that we learn something about Waugh himself. When he came down from Oxford, Waugh had in mind to be a man of letters. His *Rossetti* (1928) and *Edmund Campion* (1935), which won the Hawthornden prize, quite apart from his first four novels *Decline and Fall*, *Vile Bodies*, *Black Mischief* and *A Handful of Dust*, had taken him some way towards fulfilling that aspiration before he set out for the Abyssinian war.

The journalists he consorted with in Addis Ababa could by no stretch of the imagination be described as men of letters. The British newspapers, with one or two exceptions, took the prospect of war between Mussolini's Italy and Abyssinia less seriously than the Americans, and simply sent reporters like me to cover eventualities. Although the Americans dispatched several heavyweight foreign correspondents, none of them could be described as literary figures. Thus, from the outset, Waugh found himself a somewhat isolated figure; more famous than any of his fellow correspondents in the field, but less practised than his rivals at finding and composing the sort of stories popular newspapers wanted to print.

This division comes out sharply in his relations with Stuart Emeny of the *News Chronicle*, who does not feature in *Scoop* but of whom Waugh wrote uncharitably in his earlier book *Waugh in Abyssinia* and in letters to friends at home. It is true that Emeny represented a Liberal newspaper and Waugh at that time looked upon Mussolini favourably as a civilizing influence in a savage country. But that was not the barrier between them. I had encountered Emeny on earlier assignments in Britain. He was an experienced reporter, at one time the *News Chronicle*'s chief reporter and compared with someone like myself a big hitter. Because the three of us shared the same quarters, we came to know each other well, but Waugh, who had travelled out on the same boat as Emeny, never lost a certain contempt for him. Of the voyage itself he had written (while practising on the typewriter given to him by the *Daily Mail*) to his future wife Laura Herbert: 'This is a very decent ship but the people very dull all French colonials except for another journalist going to Abyssinia, called Emeny you will think I have spelled that wrong but no it is his name. He is a married man and does not want much to be killed and has a gas mask and a helmet and a medicine chest twice the size of all my luggage and I have told him so often that he is going to certain death that I have begun to believe it myself.'

In *Waugh in Abyssinia*, poor Emeny gets a second broadside which I have mentioned before but which, in assessing Waugh, is worth giving in full:

> I saw him constantly throughout the succeeding months and found his zeal and industry a standing reproach. I did not know it was possible for a human being to identify himself so precisely with the interests of his employers. He never stopped working; he was constantly jotting things down in a little notebook; all events for him had only one significance and standard of measurement – whether or no they constituted a 'story'. He did not make friends; he 'established contacts'. Even his private opinions were those of his paper; the situation, obscure to most of us, was crystal clear to him – the Emperor was an oppressed anti-fascist. His editor had told him that he must wear silk pyjamas under his clothes if he wished to avoid typhus. He never neglected to do so. He carried with him everywhere an iodine pencil with which he painted flea bites and scratches, so that he soon presented a somewhat macabre piebald spectacle.

[I have no recollection of this.] In the final reckoning he probably sent back sounder information than many of us.

Despite that last graceful qualification, Waugh's irritation with Emeny was always uppermost.

Waugh and Emeny were travelling together in the boat which at Port Said picked up Francis Rickett, who provided the only real scoop of the war. Rickett and the coded messages that arrived for him aroused the suspicions of both Waugh and Emeny. Waugh thought he was an arms merchant but, as I have described above, set about discovering more about him in a desultory fashion by dispatching a letter to Penelope Betjeman.

Long before Waugh could reasonably hope to receive a reply, Rickett had concluded his business in Addis Ababa and departed. Though he gave the full text of his agreement with the Emperor only to Jim Mills of Associated Press of America and Sir Percival Phillips of *The Daily Telegraph*, Rickett also took the trouble to wake up Stuart Emeny and give him the gist of the story. So Emeny got his share of the spoils for the *News Chronicle*. If Waugh had been in Addis Ababa at the time, he too might have had a corner at this feast and his career with the *Daily Mail* might have taken a different course, but he was out of reach, working on another, less sensational, story in Harar. The Count Maurice de Roquefeuil du Bousquet and his wife, an obscure couple living outside Jijiga, had been arrested, allegedly for giving information to Italian officers. Waugh and Patrick Balfour got exclusives on this, cabled their stories and returned to Addis Ababa in high spirits, reckoning they had done pretty well. But instead of the congratulations came angry cables demanding, 'What do you know Anglo-American oil concession?'

I do not think that it was Emeny's relative success and his own failure that affected Waugh's relations with Emeny. The three of us remained fairly close and Waugh taught us both to ride. We breakfasted together and sometimes compared notes. The truth is that socially Emeny was simply not Waugh's cup of tea; he did not belong to the world that Waugh liked to inhabit. Nor emphatically did the reporters and photographers who had been sent out to Abyssinia by the *Daily Express*, *Daily Graphic* and *Daily Sketch*. They form the composite characters of Corker, Shumble, Whelper and Pigge who lived in such disorder in the Hotel Liberty, spoke like cockneys and were good at their craft. I travelled back to England with one of them, a photographer called Tovey. One night on the boat I was seized with sharp stomach pains. I summoned Tovey who roused the ship's doctor – doctors on the Messageries Maritimes were not easily roused – and stayed with me until he was sure I was better. Though ostensibly there was fierce rivalry between reporters, there was also a kinship which Waugh had no wish to share. He found Stuart Emeny's anxiety about air raids and poisonous bugs bourgeois and irritating. The Reuters man, a member of the publishing family of Collins was, by Waugh standards, pretty well connected; so was his assistant, Dick Sheepshanks, an old Etonian. But I don't think Waugh bothered to meet either of them. They were not sufficiently 'amusing'.

Nor did he show much interest in the *Times* man George Steer, though he had himself been with *The Times* in 1930. In his novel, Waugh saddles what he calls the *Twopence*, which is plainly *The Times*, with a correspondent called Pappenhacker. Mr Salter had filled in William Boot on Pappenhacker, 'the cleverest man in Fleet Street'. They were dining together at the Savoy in London, where Pappenhacker was seen to quarrel with the waiters. 'He's always like that,' says Salter to Boot. 'You see he's a communist. Most staff of the *Twopence* are – they're University men, you see. Pappenhacker says that every time you are polite to a proletarian you are helping to bolster up the capitalist system . . .'

George Steer was not a man likely to attract Waugh's admiration. A short, slight man of twenty-five, he was a South African who had won scholarships to Winchester and Oxford, where he took a double first in classics. 'A zealous young colonial reporter,' was how Waugh described him, but he did better than most of us. Having reached Addis Ababa in July, ahead of the pack, he quickly became acquainted with the Emperor with whom, unlike Waugh, he was in sympathy. During an interview with Steer in July, the Emperor made it clear he expected *The Times* to acquaint its readers with his position.

Their relationship paved the way for Steer to visit the southern front, where most people expected the war to start, in August. He was allowed to see the state of Abyssinian readiness, and reported his findings directly to the Emperor after his return in September, which provided another interview. It was perhaps well for the rest of us that *The Times* did not promote Steer's copy as they might have done today. They failed to exploit the bounty which his relations with the Emperor granted them.

Steer also cultivated good relations with Margarita de Herrero, the attractive correspondent of *Le Journal* in Paris, whom he met soon after she arrived with a friend from a Spanish newspaper. George and Margarita married in Addis Ababa in May 1936 as the war (which Steer reported from start to finish) was ending. After she died, he married Esme Barton, daughter of the British minister in Addis Ababa and – though Waugh insisted otherwise – the alleged model for Basil Seal's girlfriend, Prudence, in *Black Mischief*. Stuart Emeny was killed in action less than a decade later, in his fortieth year. Sent to cover General Orde Wingate and his Chindits working 200 miles behind the lines in Burma, he died in the aircraft which crashed into a mountainside and also killed Wingate.

The only man with a name comparable to Pappenhacker in Addis Ababa was H. R. Knickerbocker, one of Randolph Hearst's stars and the most enterprising of the American contingent. Waugh mocked him in private – as he mocked all the Americans there – but they got on reasonably well until, as I have recounted, Knickerbocker after a friendly game of poker implied that Waugh as a novelist came second in his esteem to Aldous Huxley.

One of the funniest characters in *Scoop* was not based on anyone in Abyssinia at all. This is the legendary Wenlock Jakes who had scooped the world with an eyewitness story of the *Lusitania* four hours before she was hit. Sent to report a revolution in the Balkans, he had fallen asleep in the train, got out at the wrong capital but dispatched such a vivid portrait of civil war that fighting actually broke out. Waugh has Jakes in his spare time writing a book called *Under the Ermine* for which he was to receive an advance of $20,000 – in those days comparable to some of the breathtaking publishing deals we read of today.

Jakes is drawn from Johnny Gunther of the Chicago *Daily News*, who caught the public eye with a remarkably successful book first published in 1936 – which was revised and republished several times – called *Inside Europe*. It made its first appearance while Waugh was slowly writing *Scoop*, and was the sort of book that set Waugh's satirical whiskers twitching. 'I shall never forget,' he has Jakes writing, 'the evening of King Edward's abdication. I was dining at the Savoy Grill as the guest of Silas Shock of the *New York Guardian*. His guests were well chosen, six of the most influential men and women in England, who are seldom in the news but who control the strings of the national purse . . .' In another excerpt, Jakes is found writing, 'The Archbishop of Canterbury who, it is well known, is behind Imperial Chemicals . . .' Authentic Gunther.

By an odd coincidence the Chicago *Daily News* man in Abyssinia was Bill Stoneman, an able correspondent who had succeeded Johnny Gunther as head of the newspaper's London bureau. When we all returned to London Stoneman and I occasionally met for lunch and he talked to me about the problems Gunther had created for him. Some of *Inside Europe* (or *Under the Ermine*) had been gathered at influential dinner tables in London and as a result Stoneman found a number of important people in London cautious about inviting him to join their parties.

The most recognizable figure from Fleet Street in *Scoop* is Sir Jocelyn Hitchcock, Waugh's portrait of Sir Percival Phillips. Phillips, an experienced and accomplished hand, had covered the Spanish–American War in Cuba for the *Telegraph* in 1898 and was one of the five accredited correspondents with the British armies on the Western Front during the First World War, for which he had been knighted. He did a short spell with the *Daily Express* and in 1924 had joined the *Daily Mail*. In 1930, while Waugh was reporting the Emperor's coronation in Addis Ababa for *The Times*, *Daily Express* and *Daily Graphic*, Phillips was the *Mail*'s star turn. Haile Selassie, who wanted to make his mark in the world with his coronation, was delighted to have someone as renowned as Phillips reporting it. Phillips attended the coronation not as a mere reporter but as the Emperor's guest. He was granted an exclusive interview during which Phillips was entrusted with a 'special message . . . for the people of the British Empire'. But Phillips also sent the *Telegraph* a colourful and accurate account of the coronation ceremony which (in common with many other accounts) was 'delayed in transmission'.

Then, after a difference with Rothermere and possibly disenchanted with the erratic policies of the *Daily Mail*, he returned to *The Daily Telegraph*, where one of his first assignments was to cover the Italian invasion of Abyssinia. That is why, after losing Phillips, the *Mail* was willing to employ Waugh for the crisis of 1935 and why there was such bitterness there when Phillips secured his Rickett scoop for the *Telegraph*, leaving Waugh and the *Daily Mail* empty-handed. Because he was in Harar when the story broke, a whole day's journey from the capital, Waugh was not even in a position to 'follow up speediest'. Perhaps too much has been made of this in the past by some of us writing about Waugh, and on reflection I am not sure how much it counted in the long run. It soured relations, indeed ultimately terminated them, between Waugh and the *Daily Mail*. It also brought to a close Waugh's profitable custom of securing a two-book contract for an event, then getting a newspaper to employ him and pay his expenses; but that system was almost certainly coming to an end anyway. It had worked for Haile Selassie's coronation in 1930 and it served in 1935–6. While Waugh's style of living exceeded his income it was useful, but Waugh's career was moving on. Other doors were opening to him.

There are other characters in the book I recognize. The Swede, his eccentricity concealing a big heart concerned with relieving human suffering, was there. So was the wild Spaniard. So was Popotakis, who ran one of Addis Ababa's nightclubs, and in *Scoop* a ping-pong parlour. Waugh claimed to have discussed with him how much he and his wife enjoyed flagellation, but one took that sort of talk from Waugh with a pinch of salt. The Frenchmen and the rows they created at angry meetings of the Foreign Press Association are true to life. Dr Benito, director of the press bureau, who so infuriated us, appears in *Scoop* exactly as he was in real life. Improbably too, Excelsior Movie-Sound News of America, its team captained by the flamboyant playwright Lawrence Stallings, existed. Come to think of it, a junior member of that outfit was much smitten by a cool German huntress whom we encountered. She wore white silk shirts. Perhaps she inspired Waugh's Katchen, though I think it unlikely. Waugh's sketches in *Scoop* convey very well the assortment of improbable people drawn to Abyssinia by the war.

Jack Bannister of the British legation, who put William Boot on the right trail, was very much there in 1935. Emeny and I made the acquaintance of such a man and he provided us with some good copy. Assistance was mutual. The legation staff knew we employed local men – 'spies' Waugh rather grandly called them – and valued the gossip they brought us. Because of Waugh's low standing at the legation, where the shadow of Prudence and *Black Mischief* hung over him, he was exiled from such confidences, and, to be fair, he did not seek them.

To some readers, *Scoop* confirms the impression that Waugh was a successful novelist but a failed newspaper reporter. Behind the banter, they reason, we find a man poking fun at a profession that humiliated him. He takes his revenge on those who outclassed him in the newspaper business by lampooning them and with a storyline which has them all outwitted by a country hick. It is not an unreasonable interpretation of *Scoop*, and I plead guilty to giving it some support in years past when writing about Waugh. Indeed, Waugh himself leads us in that direction. Consider the passage in the letter to Penelope Betjeman from Abyssinia already mentioned: 'I am a very bad journalist . . .' and also the letter to Katharine Asquith quoted on page 29.

If Waugh considered himself a failed reporter, who are we to contradict him? Yet I have come to see that the obvious interpretation is the wrong one; Waugh in fact had the qualities of a good reporter. His ear was well attuned to the idiocies of this world. He was curious, thorough in any enquiry he made, very quick on the uptake, persistent and observant, and never nervous of embarrassing anyone. Only a good reporter could have wrung so many secrets from the undertakers before writing *The Loved Ones*. Because Waugh's relations with the *Daily Mail* broke down over the Rickett affair soon after he got to Abyssinia, the copy he sent the newspaper thereafter is not an altogether fair test of his abilities.

A fairer measurement is what he had written five years earlier from Abyssinia when reporting the coronation. While writing an introduction to the Folio Society's edition of *Black Mischief*, I persuaded *The Times* library to trace some of this for me. It took some doing because there were few bylines in those days and Waugh's copy is anonymous, from 'our special correspondent'. But it is unquestionably what newspapers call 'a good read', less detailed than Sir Percival Phillips's copy in *The Daily Telegraph* but more colourful and more accurate than almost all the other accounts. Because communications were so slow, some reporters filed their stories before the coronation took place, so their descriptions of what took place were perforce wildly inaccurate.

Waugh had something to say about this practice of describing events in advance in his chapter about the coronation in *Remote People*. 'It was highly interesting,' he wrote, 'when the papers began to arrive from Europe and America, to compare my own experiences with those of different correspondents . . . It seemed to me that we had been witnesses of a quite different series of events. "Getting in first with the news" and "giving the public what it wants", the two dominating principles of Fleet Street, are not always reconcilable.' In Addis Ababa, Waugh declares, he was able to watch the machinery of journalism working in a simplified form. 'A London office is too full and complicated to enable one to form opinions . . . Here I knew most of the facts and people involved, and in the light of this knowledge I found the Press reports shocking and depressing.'

My journalist friends will claim that Waugh's observations simply confirm how totally unsuited he was to be a reporter. I am not entering that argument, only suggesting that Waugh's disenchantment with the modern press did not spring simply from his failure to please the *Daily Mail* in Abyssinia in 1935; it sprang more from observing the antics of some of his colleagues there in 1930. *Scoop* is not an expression of Waugh's disappointment with himself. It is a send-up of a world he judged to be irredeemably slipshod and pretentious.

Eight

Sixty-five years after the *Morning Post* recalled me from Addis Ababa, leaving the rest of the war to newspapers with deeper purses, *The Daily Telegraph* asked me to return to report the funeral of Haile Selassie I, Emperor of Abyssinia. It was an unusual event in that not many men are ceremoniously buried a quarter of a century after their death. A prisoner in his own palace after being deposed by the armed forces in 1974, the Emperor had died there on 27 August 1975 at the age of eighty-three. The cause of death was reported officially as circulatory failure; most people were in no doubt that he had been murdered.

The complex and bloody process whereby, after ten years of military rule, a workers' party on the Soviet model was formed with Lieutenant Colonel Mengistu Haile Mariam as general secretary, forms a small part of this story. Marxism was on the march in many parts of Africa at that time and in Ethiopia its principal advocate was Mengistu, who went on to become president when the People's Democratic Republic of Ethiopia was established in 1987. Aware of the Soviet Union's ambitions in Africa and hopeful of support, he sought to ally himself with the Russians and for a while turned the country from a feudal state into a Marxist one.

I caught a whiff of his ruthless power while on a visit to Ethiopia in 1988. My successor as editor of *The Daily Telegraph*, Max Hastings, had suggested I go back and look up some of my old haunts from 1935. Addis Ababa had grown into a very different place since my first acquaintance with it. There were still flocks of goats and sheep being driven along its main streets, but now they had to compete with cars and lorries. From a rough camp of 100,000 people at the time of the Emperor's coronation in 1930 it had become a diplomatic centre and the home of the Organization for African Unity. This prominence was due partly to the railway from the coast, completed in 1929, and partly to the communications created by the Italians during their brief occupation. But in 1988 an air of menace hung over the place. It was in the grip of militant Marxism, with archways displaying slogans such as 'Long Live Proletarian Internationalism'. Even in the relative sanctuary of the Hilton, life was severely circumscribed. To go anywhere, you had to order your taxi at a desk in the hotel, enter full particulars of where you were going and whom you wished to see. On arrival at your destination, the taxi disappeared. To return to base, you had to telephone the hotel and ask for another taxi out to fetch you back. Visiting 'old haunts' in Addis Ababa was an expensive exercise.

The Italians had not remained long enough to leave the distinguishing marks they had placed on Asmara, with its modern cathedral, palm-lined main avenue and fine villas. However, they had bequeathed Addis one or two good restaurants and built new roads which meant that the capital was no longer dependent on the railway as its sole lifeline. Until the Italians arrived, Abyssinian's rulers had believed that roads would open the country up to invaders and had stuck to tracks. But Addis Ababa itself remained an untidy town, with a few old palaces and churches but virtually no modern building of distinction. My impression, drawn from Eastern Europe, had been that communists were rather good at preserving ancient buildings; this seemed not to apply to Mengistu's brand of Marxism. A statue of Lenin donated by Moscow in 1984 to mark the founding of the Workers' Party of Ethiopia had but a brief life. In 1991 a young artist painted the crowd pulling it down. It was then dumped on the edge of the city.

With difficulty, I obtained permission to visit the ancient city of Harar, via Dire Dawa, on the railway. I wanted to renew my acquaintance with that remarkable feat of engineering. The train ride is worth the journey if only to cross the gorge at Awash. I speculated on how many lives had been lost driving the line through that rugged country over the mountains up to Addis Ababa. Throughout the journey I was accompanied by a young guide whose job it was to ensure that I did not stray from the prescribed path, take photographs or note military movements. He eventually became stupefied chewing *kat*, which he picked up at one of the railway stations, but that was not until we were on the return train to Addis Ababa.

Waugh in 1935 had found the city disappointing compared with 1930; by 1988 it had sunk further into decay. The only entertainment on offer was the hyena man, who went to the outskirts of the city every evening with a bucket of raw meat and called the hyenas. As they slunk in, he encouraged them to come closer by throwing chunks of meat only a few feet away. So the entertainment consisted of watching a pack of hyenas scrabble for stinking meat close to your feet. It well fitted the state of Ethiopia in the year 1988.

At home or abroad, I favour a brisk morning walk for the good of my health. In the Addis Ababa of Major Mengistu Haile Mariam, this became a hazardous undertaking. All pedestrians were suspect and European pedestrians were made to feel a threat to the safety of the state. Guards outside buildings one stopped to look at clicked their rifle bolts and conveyed with menacing body language that you were unwelcome and would do well to move on. It was partly this experience that led me to share with many others the darkest doubts about the circumstances of the Emperor's death.

Ethiopia, whose people I have come to admire, was extremely unfortunate to have Mengistu in charge for any length of time; he was brutal but he was also second-rate. There were many people in Ethiopia capable of running that complicated country better than him; but that is the nature of revolution. Serious food shortages in several parts of Ethiopia first became apparent in 1982 and 1983; by 1984 there was famine. Drought had contributed to the problem, but it was the sweeping land reforms instituted by the Derg (as Mengistu's group of cut-throats was called) that did most of the damage.

At first Mengistu found it convenient to do nothing about the situation; he appeared to think that hungry people might be less eager to support the burgeoning guerrilla movements. Then pictures began to appear on Western television screens of starving peasants, abandoned homesteads and dying beasts. The Derg, driven to admit that a serious crisis existed, at first accused Western relief organizations of negligence. That was when Bob Geldof's Band Aid sprang into existence. 'Do They Know It's Christmas?' echoed across the world. I heard the concert while waiting for a flight in the airport at Kuala Lumpur. Scores of passengers crowded round the screens, aware that something unusual was going on.

The imposition of a Soviet-style collective farm system on Abyssinia's peasantry was a catastrophe but it also spelt the beginning of the end for Mengistu. His most dangerous enemies were the guerrilla movements in Eritrea and Tigre. By the close of the 1980s they had scored spectacular victories against Mengistu's armies and had developed close ties with the United States. On 21 May 1991, Mengistu slipped out of the capital in a small plane, ostensibly to visit training camps in the south. The pilot was then ordered to fly over the Kenyan border and land at Nairobi. From there Mengistu flew to Harare, where Mugabe, alone among African leaders, proved willing to grant him asylum. During those hideous years 70,000 Ethiopians had left the country seeking a more rewarding life in the United States of America. They were the fortunate ones; tens of thousands died needlessly.

After Mengistu had taken refuge with Mugabe (and returning to my part in the story), a search began for the Emperor's remains. It proved a daunting task, for Mengistu's men had buried the body secretly. They had chosen a bathroom next to Mengistu's office in the palace and had dug a hole nine feet deep in the floor. Into this the Emperor's corpse was placed vertically, and the space above him then filled with concrete. It took the search party a day to work their way through this with a pneumatic drill, but the remains were finally exhumed on 17 February 1992. Small wonder the story got about that Mengistu had arranged for the Emperor's corpse to be buried under his lavatory. It was apparently true.

Salvaged from Mengistu's bathroom, the remains were then moved to a monastery and a committee of the Emperor's admirers began very slowly to plan a proper burial for his remains in the royal mausoleum of Trinity Cathedral in Addis Ababa. At first they hoped also to establish scholarship and library projects as a memorial, but such plans proved financially out of reach. The next step in this slow-moving saga was setting up the Emperor Haile Selassie I Memorial Foundation in 1995. Seeking to give him a state funeral to which world leaders would be invited, the foundation wrote a long letter to the prime minister of the Ethiopian republic requesting this. Reluctant to revive royalist sentiments, the government resisted a state event but consented to the elaborate burial ceremony in Addis Ababa which I was to witness. November 2000 was seen as an appropriate date, coming seventy years after the Emperor's coronation in 1930.

News of these plans reached me via the long arm of coincidence. Sir Conrad Swan, Garter King of Arms, planned to attend the ceremony for among the Emperor's numerous honours and awards was the Garter. Haile Selassie also held the Royal Victorian Chain which, the gift of the monarch, confers no precedence on its holders and is confined almost exclusively to royalty and heads of state. In addition, Britain had given him the honorary rank of field marshal, an honorary GCB and a GCMG. On a portrait of him in full military dress I once counted fourteen rows of medals – fifty-seven in all – which, as I wrote at the time, might well have qualified him for the *Guinness Book of Records*. Swan wrote to Conrad Black, proprietor of *The Daily Telegraph* and a fellow Canadian, asking if he might report the event for us. Conrad passed the letter on to Charles Moore, the editor. He, knowing of my past, asked if I would care to do the job. Over a convivial lunch at Wilton's, Swan passed the baton over to me. So for the fifth time in my life, though in swifter transport and with less luggage than in 1935, I set off for Addis Ababa. Under any dispensation it takes time to find out what is happening in that capital. The newspaper had received no formal invitation to the ceremony and I was not sure how welcome we would be. Abbie Trayler-Smith, the *Telegraph* photographer who came with me, agreed that we should give ourselves plenty of time to look round and this proved to be as well.

'Goodness,' I wrote in my column later, 'how hard it is to adjust to "African time" – and how good it is for you.' Arriving in Ethiopia, or almost anywhere else in Africa, one tends to expect everything to happen at the pace at which we now drive ourselves in the industrial West. 'Where's the car I ordered twenty minutes ago?' 'Car is coming.' 'Yes, but when, for heaven's sake?' 'Car come soon.' Once you bring yourself to accept the tempo with good grace, slow down and get into step, it all works wonderfully well and you feel refreshed. With 'African time' in mind, I thought we should leave ourselves three clear days before the main event. What a happy experience it was on entering my room at the Hilton to plug in my laptop, realize there would be no queue at the cable station and that my copy would cost *The Daily Telegraph* a lot less than today's equivalent of half a crown a word.

Abbie had discovered the address and telephone number of the Haile Selassie I Memorial Foundation. Tracking it down was another story. Our taxi swirled about in the Addis traffic as we peered into unlikely windows. 'Enough of this,' I said eventually. At 11.35 a.m. we went to the department of information seeking fresh bearings. Everyone was at lunch, they said, until 1.30 p.m. 'Come back then.' Vintage Evelyn Waugh, I thought. Then, after our driver had done some telephoning, we finally tracked down the foundation. It occupied a small single room off a cul-de-sac, where a courteous couple presented us with passes for Sunday's ceremony and a letter of credentials. It crossed my mind that, though clearly sanctioned by the Ethiopian government, this event was in the hands of private enterprise, so to consolidate our position, we returned to the department of information, which occupied shabby quarters at the top of a steep stone staircase. A formidable Ethiopian woman called for our letter of authority. Half asleep by then, I assumed she was seeking something we had omitted to get from the *Telegraph*. Despairingly, I offered to get it faxed from London. While we wrangled, Abbie produced the letter of credentials from the foundation, which I had forgotten. Happy smiles. We were in!

For our next move, I suggested to Abbie, we should try something less strenuous. 'Let's see if we can find the old Imperial Hotel,' I said, 'where the newspapermen slept four to a room in 1935.' 'Yes, driver he knows,' declared our taxi man confidently. We fetched up outside a large modern hotel. 'Is this what you remember?' asked Abbie drily. No, it was not. We made further enquiries. Ah, they said, the hotel you want is now called the Itegue Taitu. I learned for the first time that it had been built nearly one hundred years before by the Empress Taitu, and had been the country's first hotel. It seemed to me little changed from 1935, and had fallen on hard times. It had kept all its dark brown paint and inside was the old piano round which the reporters sometimes had sung. The bedroom floor, each of its rooms behind double doors, was deserted. As we strolled round, a young Frenchman appeared called Lefort, who had just taken over the hotel with grand plans in mind. The place would be restored, he explained, and become an arts centre. There would be space for lectures, a recording studio and bedrooms for guest artists. Ethiopia being richer in old treasures than any other African country I know, though the visitor rarely sets eyes on them, this seemed a good idea.

We seemed to be on a winning streak. I suggested to Abbie a light lunch, a tour of the route the ceremony would be taking on Sunday and then, as we had been flying all the previous night, a siesta. We dined that evening in the Hilton's swish Jacaranda room, where an orchestra softly played 'The Way We Were' and then 'My Way'. You have to go abroad and to fairly remote countries to hear that sort of thing nowadays, I explained to Abbie. I thought of the extraordinarily squalid nightclub to which Waugh and I had occasionally resorted in 1935. The memory doubled the pleasure of every mouthful of food and sip of wine at the Hilton but left me with the same nagging worry that I had felt sixty-five years earlier: where was I going to find the copy to justify my expenses?

We set about easing that anxiety early the next morning. The *Telegraph* wanted a preliminary story and I had woken with the thought that a great many ghosts would be walking in Addis Ababa as the capital prepared for Sunday's events. One of them would be that of Sir Sidney Barton, British minister at the legation between 1929 and 1936. By the year 2000 this was of course an embassy, but our ambassador there since 1997, Gordon Wetherell, was no longer in residence. Though a fluent speaker of Amharic, he had just been transferred to Luxembourg. So we decided not to go to the British embassy but to visit the railway station, revisit the foundation and then try to get photographs of the tomb awaiting the Emperor's remains.

The railway and its station, Chemin de Fer: Djibouti-Ethiopien, that miracle of French engineering, looked exactly as it had in 1935. At first we were followed by a man with a rifle, who made us nervous, but subsequently we fell into the right hands and were ushered into the presence of the stationmaster himself. Nobody believed for a moment that I had been there in 1935, but they were wonderfully polite and nodded indulgently at my recollections, passing them off as the delusions to which old men are prone. Back at the foundation, we were treated as old friends and given a copy of the programme for Sunday, all of it in Amharic. Then to the cathedral and another stroke of luck: a guide showed our letter of authority to the priest, who granted us entry to the inner sanctuary, the thrones and the open tomb. Great pictures and good copy. In return for these privileges I disbursed money freely, for which the recipients looked even more grateful than we felt.

In the story I sent to the *Telegraph* that evening, I recalled my last meeting with the Emperor at Prince's Gate in London in 1936:

> His aides had intoned: 'We have never desired war. It was imposed upon us . . . devastated fields and ruined villages . . . the bodies of the aged and of the women . . . and children. Cannot in silence and indifference be destroyed without subjecting humanity to the triumph and rule of force over right.'
>
> Oh God, I thought, recalling those words – how often have we all heard them intoned since? But the Lion of Judah as he was called fell early in what we now recognize as an overture to the Second World War.

In his account of the coronation in *Remote People*, Waugh describes the Emperor's all-night vigil before his coronation and his own very early rising for the ceremony. There had been an echo of that, I reported, on the previous Thursday morning, 1 November, anniversary of the coronation, when hundreds in Addis Ababa had turned out long before the chilly dawn to attend requiem mass at the seventy Orthodox churches in the capital.

I think, I told Abbie over breakfast on Saturday, that this is a day for a short break in the countryside and a glimpse of Ethiopia's amazingly rich bird life. I know next to nothing about birds, but I have long been aware that the countries of east Africa display a richer variety of them than most places and when I am there I try to see a little of it. So, off to a lake outside Addis Ababa, where there were herons in abundance, for a recharging of the batteries before Sunday's ceremonies, which I anticipated would keep us at full stretch for about six hours.

The foundation had decided that Sunday's ceremony should be spread over three places of worship with which the Emperor had been associated. Try to imagine a ceremony, I explained to readers of the newspaper, which starts with the removal of royal remains from, say, St Peter's in Eaton Square, where the first service is held. Then the cortège moves to Parliament Square, where speeches are made. An hour later it stops at Westminster Abbey, where a second service is held; then finally to St Paul's Cathedral where, after a third service, the remains are finally entombed. That is roughly what was to happen in Addis Ababa that Sunday morning. We shall need a reliable driver, I thought, as we put our preparations in hand.

Shortly before 8 a.m. we joined a large crowd outside Bahata church, where the great Menelik II had been buried. As we arrived we could hear over the loudspeakers the Lord's

Prayer in Amharic. Women outside the church were circling round in tears, crying, 'Our master, our master.' There were old soldiers in shabby tunics, sola topis and lopsided medals, some of them shedding manly tears. Yet, as I also reported at the time, young men were there too, sensing perhaps that something from the past was passing for ever.

Dignitaries of the Orthodox Church were present in abundance, gorgeously robed, their dignity sadly impaired by the chaotic tangle of microphones, cameras and film crews which surrounded them. What sport Waugh would have had, I reflected, with this bizarre mixture of the sacred and profane. In Western capitals we have learned how to tame the modern news media at major events. After years of singularly grey regimes, Addis Ababa had no experience of the rota system, whereby one or two cameramen and reporters are admitted to events on condition their work is passed on to everyone else. Like the Emperor's coronation seventy years earlier, this burial was an unprecedented event. The government played the game in permitting it to occur, but took no hand in the arrangements. The Foundation had no authority to enforce its own arrangements and later that day we would witness even worse scenes of media free-for-all. So it was with difficulty that we heard the Patriarch, engulfed by the media, declare, 'It was a democratic act to bury him properly. He contributed much to what Ethiopia is today and he has made the Orthodox Church known throughout the world.'

They beat a great drum, which I had last heard in October 1935 as war with Italy began. There was much solemn chanting as ceremonial spears flashed in the sunlight and a splendid bodyguard surrounded the Emperor's coffin. This was on a decorated lorry. Where, I wondered, had they kept all those splendid robes during Ethiopia's dark years? The chairman of the foundation spoke: 'He was a good emperor. Everyone is thinking about his reign. If we believe in God, the Emperor will not forget Ethiopia. There has been much confusion, but we have succeeded in the end . . .' I spoke to an old soldier of eighty-seven who had been wounded in the Congo. He was wondering if his damaged leg would last the day.

After an hour and a half of this, we moved on to Meskel Square. There were more speeches and the crowd following the cortège had grown. It suddenly occurred to me that at this rate proceedings might not end before my copy was expected in London. While Abbie set out to get pictures of the scene, I sat in the back of our taxi and began scribbling. Eventually, as noon approached, we moved on to St George's church for further obsequies; it was here that the Emperor had been crowned in 1930. For the funeral they had wound round its hexagonal walls a huge sash in the Ethiopian colours of red, yellow and green. I watched the scene from a safe distance while Abbie found perilous perches from which to get her pictures. As Waugh would certainly have observed, it was a grand day for hawkers, beggars, cripples and small children, who sought alms at every turn in the proceedings.

The sun had begun to turn down by the time we reached Holy Trinity cathedral, which had been built at the Emperor's behest and where his remains would lie in a tomb alongside his Empress. The main service was being held outside the cathedral, so the VIPs, most of them from embassies, were seated on the steps of the cathedral entrance, where they had slowly roasted in the tropical sun. Having thoughtlessly set out without a hat that morning, I sought a corner in the shade under the cathedral wall and gave my feet a rest. To my shame, the enterprising Abbie, who had been lugging round heavy camera equipment all morning, came to advise me that there was plenty of space inside the cathedral. She thought it might be a good plan to move inside while we had a chance. It was timely advice. Knowing this would be the final phase of the proceedings, the largest crowd of all had gathered round the cathedral. Many had been there since dawn and it was now approaching 2 p.m.

We squeezed through the main entrance to find the local news media everywhere. Abbie and I were among the few drawn to this event from the outside world. The television men who occupied the pulpit were mostly local stringers aiming to make a bob or two. Across the cathedral's altar steps and choir stall cables trailed and camera lights flashed. As relatives and distinguished visitors were being admitted, I encountered Sir Conrad, Garter King of Arms. 'To deliver the sacred to the masses,' I murmured to him, 'involves an unholy mess!' He gave me a friendly but bewildered smile. Thanks to our reconnaissance two days earlier, Abbie and I had a fair idea of where it was best to sit. With notebook or camera in one hand and our shoes in the other, we occupied a pew directly behind the inner sanctuary, across which curtains had been lightly drawn.

As the cortège arrived at its final destination, drums beat

and a great bell tolled. The coffin was carried in by eight pall-bearers, followed by the bodyguard. Abbie took a peep through the curtain and reported to me that, unknown to the congregation, the pall-bearers were having difficulty fitting the coffin into the open tomb. Goodness, I thought, what would Evelyn Waugh make of that! There was an interval as they worked on it. A chair was brought for the Emperor's only surviving child, Princess Tenangne Work, a woman in her seventies, who briefly delivered an address. Behind the closed curtains to which we were closer than anyone else and through which Abbie had peered, we could guess what was going on. It was a tight fit; the coffin was almost the same size as the interior of the tomb. But in the end they managed it.

I glanced at my service paper, on which the last words were taken from 2 Timothy 4: 7–8. They ran: 'I have fought the good fight. I have finished the race. I have kept the faith. Finally, there is laid up for me the crown of righteousness, which the Lord, the righteous judge, will give to me on that Day, and not to me only but also to all who have loved his appearing.'

I turned to Abbie and said, 'I think it's time to go. There is copy to write, pictures to send, and there will be an almighty scrum.' We slipped out and soon found our patient taxi driver. We reached the Hilton in time for some refreshment before settling down to work. I thought of the cable station in Addis Ababa sixty-five years earlier. For the coronation in 1930, I had read, newspapers had hired crack pilots to fly the photographs across Africa to London.

In my room at the Hilton, I gave my laptop an encouraging

smile and sent London 900 words within a couple of hours. Abbie wired some brilliant pictures of the day's work in roughly the same time. The Emperor had always believed in progress.

Bibliography

The Abyssinian Difficulty, Darrell Bates. Oxford University Press.

Layers of Time, A History of Ethiopia, Paul B. Henze. Hurst & Company.

The Emperor, Ryszard Kapuściński, Quartet Books Ltd.

Haile Selassie's War, Anthony Mockler, Oxford University Press.

Remote People, Evelyn Waugh. Duckworth.

Scoop, Evelyn Waugh. Chapman & Hall Ltd.

Waugh in Abyssinia, Evelyn Waugh. Methuen.